INTERSECTORAL
CAPITAL FLOWS
IN THE ECONOMIC
DEVELOPMENT
OF TAIWAN,
1895–1960

INTERSECTORAL CAPITAL FLOWS IN THE ECONOMIC DEVELOPMENT OF TAIWAN, 1895–1960

by Teng-hui Lee

CORNELL UNIVERSITY PRESS
Ithaca and London

Copyright © 1971 by Cornell University

All rights reserved. Except for brief quotations in a review, this book, or parts thereof, must not be reproduced in any form without permission in writing from the pubisher. For information address Cornell University Press, 124 Roberts Place, Ithaca, New York 14850.

First published 1971 by Cornell University Press.
Published in the United Kingdom by Cornell University Press Ltd.,
2–4 Brook Street, London W1Y 1AA.

International Standard Book Number 0–8014–0650–1
Library of Congress Catalog Card Number 76–159031

PRINTED IN THE UNITED STATES OF AMERICA
BY KINGSPORT PRESS, INC.

TO MY WIFE

Foreword

The rate of capital accumulation plays a central role in most concepts of economic growth. The need to accumulate capital for growth is further emphasized by technological change, which is so often expressed in new forms of capital goods and provides increased returns to investment.

There is considerable variability among individuals, groups, and sectors of the economy in the extent of savings and investment. It is therefore useful to analyze the economy by sectors which differ with respect to the savings potentials and habits of the members of the sector, the investment opportunities and rates of return to investment within the sector, the way expansion of investment is organized, and the appropriateness of various means for tapping the savings pool. Growing from the heterogeneity of savings and investment conditions in various sectors is the likelihood of substantial imbalances between savings and investment within a sector. Unless these imbalances are corrected by mechanisms for transferring income and savings from one sector to another, there will be a lower aggregate rate of savings and investment and a misallocation of resources.

The agricultural sector is of particular interest and concern with respect to capital accumulation in the early stages of economic development. The agricultural sector is initially dominant in the economy; it includes the bulk of national income, labor, and capital resources. In the long run the nonagricultural sectors must grow at a substantially more rapid rate than the agricultural sector, gradually providing a transformation of the economy from one dominated by agriculture to one dominated by other sectors. It is logical to presume that this process of economic transformation will proceed more rapidly if a net transfer of income and savings can be made from the agricultural sector to other sectors of the economy.

This view of the agricultural sector as a net contributor to the capital accumulation of other sectors is widely held in the literature of economic development. There are, however, a number of controversies, not only regarding the general view of agriculture's role in industrial capital formation but also concerning a number of details, including the timing and means for facilitating such transfers.

A common argument against expecting or forcing a net contribution of income and capital toward development of other sectors is that agriculture itself has an important role to play in development through expansion of its own production, an expansion that in turn requires a large increase in the capital stock. The question is raised how the agricultural sector, in which per capita incomes are already low even by the standard of low-income countries, can provide the capital for its own expansion as well as contribute to other sectors. In recognition of the apparent conflict between the need for rapid growth of agriculture, the resultant demand for capital within the agricultural sector, and the apparent need for a transfer of capital from agriculture to other sectors, it is suggested that economic development should occur in a sequential fashion: first, substantial investment in agriculture and development of the agricultural sector, and then, from that base of agricultural development, major transfers from the agricultural to the nonagricultural sectors. In addition to a number of conceptual inconsistencies and con-flicts in such a pattern of development there seems little evi-dence that such a pattern has in fact been followed by presently developed countries. Thus a successful resolution of this difficult conflict has not been provided.

In addition to this underlying controversy, a number of questions arise as to the mechanisms by which a basically consumer-goods-producing industry like agriculture, can con-tribute to accelerated growth in the capital stock of other sectors. There are further questions about the types of trans-fer mechanisms to be used and about the problems arising in transferring income and capital from the agricultural to the nonagricultural sectors. In the face of such controversy and question, appeal to specific experience can be useful in sug-gesting resolution of conflicts, in improving our concep-tualization of this aspect of the development process, and in planning specific programs and policies for application to other countries.

The economy of Taiwan offers an unusual opportunity for study of these processes. Taiwan is a case of successful eco-nomic development. More important for the purpose of this study, overall economic development in Taiwan has been accompanied by development of a strong agricultural sector, which has experienced rapid growth in production through technological change. Thus, Taiwan presents an ideal case for viewing intersectoral capital flows as they relate to agri-cultural development. In addition, the Taiwan economy has made varying use of several devices for transferring capital from the agricultural to the nonagricultural sector, thereby providing opportunity to observe the varying play of these different devices. Most important, accurate data are avail-able for the period 1911–1960 which allow construction of a detailed set of social income accounts. For the period 1895–

1911, the data are less complete but still sufficient to allow analysis of the earliest period of accelerated economic development in Taiwan.

Teng-hui Lee has assembled a set of accounts which describe the gross and net flows of resources and income between agriculture and other sectors. He relates these flows to the processes of development of the agricultural sector itself and deals with the financial and other mechanisms required to facilitate the flows of resources among sectors. He gives attention to the difficult problem of the role of changes in relative price relationships in influencing intersectoral resource transfers. This treatment is particularly valuable because of the complex and, hence, little understood role of agricultural prices in the development process. Agricultural prices influence the allocation of resources to and within the agricultural sector and, thus, the level of agricultural production, the distribution of income among sectors of the economy and among income strata of the population, and, of course, the flow of capital resources from one sector to another. In performing their various functions, agricultural price relationships interact with other mechanisms, such as taxes and direct investment, which also influence income and capital flows. By including consideration of all the mechanisms that facilitate transfer of resources among sectors, Lee illustrates the role that agriculture may play in the development process.

Teng-hui Lee has brought to this study an intimate acquaintance with Taiwan and its various development efforts and a long period of scholarly research, both during his tenure as chief of the Agricultural Economics section of the Taiwan Provincial Department of Agriculture and Forestry and during the period subsequent to 1957 as the economist for the Sino-American Joint Commission on Rural Reconstruction. The large number of papers he has authored and coauthored include "An Analytical Review of Agricultural Development in Taiwan: An Input-Output and Productivity Approach," "Irrigation Investment in Taiwan," and "Agricultural Development and Its Contributions to Economic Growth in Taiwan." In addition, many of the statistical series which he used in this work were compiled by himself or under his direction, giving a special authority to his work with these data.

This study is part of a large program of research at Cornell University dealing with intersectoral relationships in the processes of economic development. Major work in this project has been performed with respect to the economies of Taiwan, India, and Chile, and substantial related work has been done in Pakistan, Nepal, and Thailand. Lee's work has been of enormous help in conceptualizing the approach and delineating the methods of empirical analysis. The work published here grows out of Lee's Ph.D. dissertation, which in 1969 was recognized by the American Agricultural Economics Association in its annual award for outstanding doctoral dissertations.

JOHN W. MELLOR

Ithaca, New York

Acknowledgments

Much of the statistical information upon which this book is based has been compiled from the author's research on agricultural development in Taiwan since 1957. During this period Miss Yueh-eh Chen, as my statistical assistant in the Sino-American Joint Commission on Rural Reconstruction, enthusiastically helped me with many details.

I would like to express my appreciation to Professors Kazushi Ohkawa, Shigeru Ishikawa, Bruce F. Johnston, V. W. Ruttan, John C. H. Fei, and Mr. Raymond P. Christensen for their valuable suggestions and comments in various stages of this study. I am particularly indebted to Dr. Uma J. Lele, who has carefully read and edited the manuscript, including substantive revision of Chapters 5 and 6.

Throughout the period of research connected with this study, I have benefited greatly from the advice and assistance of Professor John W. Mellor. Our continuous discussion on the basic idea behind this book has helped to bring it to completion.

Lastly, I wish to acknowledge the receipt of funds from the Department of Agricultural Economics, Cornell University, and the Agricultural Development Council, New York City, which made possible the research for this study at Cornell University.

T. H. LEE

Taipei, Taiwan

Contents

Figures

Tables

INTERSECTORAL
CAPITAL FLOWS
IN THE ECONOMIC
DEVELOPMENT
OF TAIWAN,
1895–1960

CHAPTER 1

Introduction

Two important conditions of economic development are technological change and increase in the capital stock. As production techniques are normally embodied in capital goods, it is seldom possible to achieve technological progress without increase in capital stock. Capital accumulation is thus a key to technological advance and economic growth.

A nation may generate an increase in real savings from internal sources through voluntary reduction in consumption; by involuntary additional taxation, by compulsory lending to the government, or by inflation; or, finally by absorption of underemployed labor into productive work. An increase in domestic capital stock from external sources may be achieved by an increase in imports of capital goods through foreign aid, through foreign private investment, and through restricted consumption of imports. However, an increase in real savings from external sources, as indicated by Nurkse, still depends upon domestic action.[1] For instance, if consumers increase spending on domestically produced goods when they cannot import, or if they switch imports from capital goods to consumer goods when additional imports of capital goods are being made by foreign aid and foreign private investment, the increase in imports of capital goods

[1] Ragnar Nurkse, *Problems of Capital Formation in Underdeveloped Countries* (Oxford: Basil Blackwell, 1955), pp. 140–141.

will be offset by reduced domestic investment. Contribution of external sources to the financing of development cannot be truly significant unless it is fitted into the domestic programs of savings and investment. The unreliability of receiving capital from foreign governments and the lack of supportive infrastructure for foreign private investment in low-income countries further complicate the problem of financing from external sources. Thus, in the less-developed countries, an increase in real savings from internal sources is of crucial importance to capital accumulation.[2]

In the less-developed countries, a large proportion of the population is engaged in subsistence agriculture, and a high proportion of the national product comes from this sector. Agriculture, therefore, is a great potential contributor to capital formation. There are two conflicting viewpoints about the capital contribution of agriculture to industrial development, views that are based primarily on different opinions of how to modernize traditional agriculture. One viewpoint is that agriculture does not require a large amount of capital for its transformation. As agriculture is the mainstay of the national economy in terms of both national product and employment, it is held that economic transformation should be accompanied by transfer of resources from agriculture to nonagriculture.[3] The other opinion is that investment requirements for agricultural transformation are so large that a net flow of capital must occur from nonagricul-

[2] John W. Mellor, *The Economics of Agricultural Development* (Ithaca, New York: Cornell University Press, 1966) , pp. 82–85.

[3] Bruce F. Johnston, "Agricultural Productivity and Economic Development in Japan," *Journal of Political Economy* (December 1951) , pp. 498–513.

ture to agriculture.[4] A synthesis of these viewpoints is suggested by Mellor:

Although a relative decline of agriculture and growth of the non-agricultural sector is inevitable in development, it does not follow that maximizing the short-run outflow of capital from agriculture will maximize the rate of economic development. Development of agriculture can contribute materially to overall economic development, and it requires a major inflow of certain forms of capital. The precise nature and size of flows of capital into and out of agriculture will depend on complex factors specific to each development situation.[5]

Obviously, there are many differences among countries in the social-institutional arrangements for mobilizing and shifting resources from the agricultural sector to the nonagricultural sector. Capital requirements for transforming traditional agriculture will also differ among countries according to the initial level of agricultural productivity and resource endowment. Thus, it is difficult to generalize about intersectoral capital flows required for the achievement of economic development, especially at short range.

The experiences of successful economic development in nineteenth-century Japan and in the twentieth-century Soviet Union have been widely quoted to support the generalization that agriculture must contribute capital to industrial

[4] V. W. Ruttan, *Considerations in the Design of a Strategy for Increasing Rice Production in Southeast Asia*, a paper presented at the Pacific Science Congress Session on Modernization of Rural Areas, Tokyo, August 27, 1966.

[5] John W. Mellor, "Toward a Theory of Agricultural Development," *Agricultural Development and Economic Growth*, ed. H. M. Southworth and Bruce F. Johnston (Ithaca, New York: Cornell University Press, 1967), p. 34.

development. The empirical studies undertaken for the two countries, however, are partial and inconsistent in method and are subject to considerable qualification.[6] This book sets forth a complete and consistent methodology for study of intersectoral capital flows and uses it for a detailed analysis of Taiwan's experience from 1895 to 1960.

The conditions in Taiwan at the commencement of its economic development were similar to the present situation facing South Asian countries. Taiwan has had unusual success in transforming its agriculture into a modern system and its total economy away from agricultural dominance.

Chapter 2 presents a statistical estimate of the intersectoral capital flows in the economy of Taiwan from 1895 to 1960. The analysis in Chapter 2 begins with the presentation of a theoretical framework for statistical measurement which is then used for analysis of intersectoral capital flows in the Taiwan economy from 1895 to 1960. The statistical procedure and sources of data are explained in detail in Appendix A.

In Chapter 3, the initial conditions of Taiwan's agriculture and the major policy components for the period 1895–1960 are investigated in order to provide a general view of

[6] For agriculture's contribution of capital to industrial development in Japan and the Soviet Union, see: Kazushi Ohkawa and Henry Rosovsky, "The Role of Agriculture in Modern Japanese Economic Development," *Economic Development and Cultural Change*, Vol. IX, No. 1, Part II (October 1960), pp. 43–67; Bruce F. Johnston, "Agricultural Productivity and Economic Development in Japan," *ibid.;* Gustav Ranis, "The Financing of Japanese Economic Development," *The Economic History Review*, Vol. XI, No. 3 (April 1959), pp. 440–454; Mellor, *The Economics of Agricultural Development*, p. 85; and Alexander Erlich, "Preobrazhenski and the Economics of Soviet Industrialization," *The Quarterly Journal of Economics*, Vol. LXIV, No. 1 (1950), pp. 57–88.

the development policy and prospects that are examined in more detail in Chapters 4 through 6.

Chapter 4 emphasizes the means by which agricultural development was successfully achieved, including types of investment in agriculture, patterns of technological change, growth rate of agricultural productivity in terms of both land and labor, and the government's role in development. An input-output approach and production-function analysis are applied to identify the means for agricultural development in the different phases.

Chapter 5 studies the process of capital flow out of agriculture with respect to the sectoral interdependence, such as demand and supply of agricultural products, government collection and disposal of agricultural products, activities of landlords in the agricultural product market, exports of agricultural commodities, and changes in sectoral terms of trade.

Chapter 6 is devoted to the analysis of financial aspects of sectoral capital flow with special emphasis on government's taxing policy and farmers' autonomous savings and investment. In this chapter, the importance of the financial transfer mechanism of capital is demonstrated by Taiwan's case.

Chapter 7 is a summary discussion of the implications of the study of Taiwan to contemporary developing nations. The economic and institutional phases that resulted from the type of sectoral capital flow in Taiwan are generalized.

This study, then, depicts the specific pattern of agricultural development that occurred in Taiwan, and attempts to account for the determinants and mechanism of net capital flow from agriculture. Through these efforts the government's strategic measures for development financing in Taiwan are identified, and what is actually important and what may be useful for the agricultural transformation in contemporary underdeveloped countries in terms of the domestic arrangement of development financing is indicated. This experience is believed to be especially relevant to the countries of South and Southeast Asia, but some of the lessons may have even wider applicability.

 CHAPTER 2

Size and Nature of the
Intersectoral Capital Flows

In the literature of economic development the measurement of intersectoral capital flows has been considered from many viewpoints among which are net savings flow, agricultural surplus, and transfer of capital.[1] The differences in approach are due, first, to differing opinions with respect to definition of what constitutes the *agricultural sector;* second, to the lack of distinction between financial and physical aspects of capital flow and lack of recognition of the relationship between the balance of income account and changes in capital account; and, third, to the difficulty of identifying the

[1] Classified as follows: (a) net savings: Kazushi Ohkawa, *Nōgyō, no keizai bunseki* (in Japanese) [Economic Analysis of Agriculture] (Tokyo: Taimeido, 1954), pp. 109–110 (hereafter referred to as *Economic Analysis of Agriculture*); and Johnston, "Agricultural Productivity and Economic Development in Japan," *op. cit.,* pp. 498–513; (b) agricultural surplus: Ragnar Nurkse, *Problems of Capital Formation in Underdeveloped Countries,* pp. 49–56; John C. H. Fei and Gustav Ranis, *Development of the Labor Surplus Economy, Theory and Policy* (Yale University: The Economic Growth Center, 1964), pp. 27–36; and Shigeru Ishikawa, *Economic Development in Asian Perspective* (Tokyo: Kinokuniya, 1967), pp. 290–347; (c) capital transfer: United Nations, Economic Commission for Asia and Far East, "Intersectoral Capital Flows in the ECAFE Countries" (unpublished report, 1963); and Ohkawa and Rosovsky, "The Role of Agriculture in Modern Japanese Economic Development," *op. cit.,* pp. 43–67.

process of transforming agricultural goods into capital goods in the course of economic development.

Framework for Measurement

The interrelationships between agricultural production and nonagricultural production are dealt with here by dividing the areas participating in the economic transactions of the national economy of Taiwan into six sectors: agricultural production, agricultural household, nonagricultural production, nonagricultural household, government, and foreign trade.

In the agricultural production sector, services of primary production factors such as land and labor flow from the agricultural household sector (D_a).[2] The sector also produces agricultural output (Y_a). The agricultural production sector consumes production goods such as chemical fertilizer, feed, and other material manufactured in the nonagricultural production sector (R^a_n). Agricultural products used in agricultural production are provided from the gross agricultural output within the sector. The net agricultural output is partially consumed by the agricultural household sector (C^a_a). The remaining amount of net output is sold to the nonagricultural production sector as raw materials (R^n_a), to the nonagricultural household sector for consumption (C^n_a), and directly to foreign trade as exports (E_a). The total quantity of agricultural products sold amounts to the sum of $R^n_a + C^n_a + E_a$. In nonagricultural production, services of production factors flow from the nonagricultural household sector (D_n). The sector produces two products, consumer

---

[2] The letters in brackets are the symbols used for the given item in the algebraic expression of these variables and relationships presented in equations below.

goods and capital goods. Consumer goods flow from the nonagricultural production sector to the nonagricultural household sector (C^n_n), to the agricultural household sector (C^a_n), to the government sector (C^g_n), and to exports (E_n). Capital goods are distributed to the agricultural production sector as intermediate goods (R^a_n), as investment goods (I_a), and for investment in its own sector (I_n). No capital goods export is assumed in this case. The government sector collects taxes (G_a) from the agricultural household sector and (G_n) from the nonagricultural household sector, and allocates the revenue for consumption of industrial goods (C^g_n), and for government savings (S_g). In the foreign trade sector, the government exports agricultural products (E_a), and industrial consumer goods (E_n), in exchange for consumer goods (M_c), and capital goods (M_i). The balance of international trade represents an additional variable (F).

Income generation is represented by flows in the opposite direction from the commodity flows between sectors. In addition to the commodity transactions between sectors, income also flows from the agricultural household sector to the nonagricultural sector in the form of payment of land rent, wages, and interest. The agricultural household sector also receives income from the nonagricultural household sector.

These commodity and income flows can be summarized in the following accounting equations:[3]

Inflows	Outflows	
$D_a + R^a_n$	$= C^a_a + C^n_a + R^n_a + E_a$	(1)
$D_n + R^n_a + M_c + M_i$	$= C^n_n + C^a_n + C^g_n + R^a_n$	(2)
	$+ I + E_n$	

[3] Fei and Ranis, *Development of the Labor Surplus Economy, Theory and Policy*, p. 57.

$$C^a_a + C^a_n + S_a + G_a = D_a \qquad (3)$$
$$C^n_a + C^n_n + S_n + G_n = D_n \qquad (4)$$
$$C^g_n + S_g = G_a + G_n \qquad (5)$$

Adding the five equations and cancelling out similar terms on both sides of the resulting equality, we have:

$$S_a + S_n + S_g = I + (E_a + E_n) - (M_c + M_i) \qquad (6)$$

or

$$I_n = (S_a - I_a) + S_n + S_g + F \qquad (7)$$

where $I = I_a + I_n$, and $F = (E_a + E_n) - (M_c + M_i)$. The terms S_a, S_n, and S_g in the above equations denote the savings of agricultural household, nonagricultural household, and government. Equation (6) is the financing equation indicating the relationship between savings and investment for the national economy as a whole. Equation (7) indicates the sectoral interdependence. The investment in the non-agricultural sector depends upon the amount of net capital flow from agriculture, size of savings in its own and government sectors, and the export surplus. Adding equations (1) and (3) for the agricultural sector, we have:

$$S_a = C^n_a + R^n_a + E_a - C^a_n - R^a_n - G_a \qquad (8)$$

As government taxing on agriculture is not greatly in the form of commodities, the term (G_a) in equation (8) may be better included in the term (S_a) from equation (8) and the term $(S_a - I_a)$ in equation (7) ; then we can draw the following cases, indicating the balance of commodity flows between agriculture and nonagriculture.

$$C^n_a + R^n_a + E_a - C^a_n - R^a_n \gtreqless I_a \qquad (9)$$

or

$$C^n_a + R^n_a + E_a - C^a_n - R^a_n - I_a = B \qquad (9')$$

The terms on the left side of equation (9′) indicate the commodity transactions between two sectors, and the term B is the balance showing the physical aspect of capital outflow from agriculture. The term B is also the balance of capital accounting between two sectors.

Generally speaking, it is more common and more useful to set up both capital and current operating (income) accounts in order to investigate the sectoral commodity and financial transactions. Capital account shows the changes in assets and liabilities. An increase in assets or decrease in liabilities indicates the outflow of capital. A decrease in assets or an increase in liabilities indicates the inflow of capital. The term B can, therefore, be expressed as follows:

$$B = R + K \qquad (10)$$

The term R on the right side of the above equation is the balance of current financial transactions between sectors, including the net payments of land rent, wages, and interest, and government taxing and subsidies. The term K is the balance of the capital account between sectors, including the net changes in outstanding short-term and long-term loans and investment.

The above exposition of the accounting system of sectoral interdependence between agriculture and nonagriculture is based on commodity and income flows and the sectoral capital accounting. The important fact is that both of the above sectoral accounts of income and capital are related to the expense accounts of income, consumption, and savings-investment in the agricultural and the nonagricultural sector. This means that the above sectoral accounts can be derived statistically from the social income accounts including income, consumption, and savings-investment in a sector. When we construct the social income account for the agricultural sector, the sectoral accounts can be systematically derived from it. The practical problems of construction of a social income account are explained in detail in Appendix A.

Equations (9') and (10) are generally valued at current prices of commodities and services in the transactions. The effects of changes in price ratios or sectoral terms of trade on sectoral capital flows are not reflected in equations (9') and (10). The term B in the equations, therefore, should be adjusted for changes in the price ratios. The equation (9') in real terms thus can be expressed:

$$(C^n_a + R^n_a + E_a) / P_a - (C^a_n + R^a_n + I_a) / P_n = B' \quad (11)$$

where P_a and P_n are price indices for agricultural products and nonagricultural products bought by the agricultural sector. When capital flows out from the agricultural sector, the term B' can be expressed:

$$B' = B/P_a + (C^a_n + R^a_n + I_a) / P_n(P_n/P_a - 1) \quad (12)$$

The first term on the right side of the equation is the financial amount of capital outflow from agriculture in real terms, and the second term is the amount of capital outflow caused by the change in the sectoral terms of trade between agriculture and nonagriculture. We call the former the visible net real capital outflow and the latter the invisible net real capital outflow.

From the above exposition on the statistical method for measuring the intersectoral capital flows, it becomes clear that the equations (11) and (12) are the most inclusive and effective ones for our study. The statistical estimates based on equations (11), (12), and the social income account of the Taiwan agriculture are summarized in Table 1.

The left side of equation (9') is used for measuring the gross outflow of agricultural products and gross inflow of

Table 1. Summary statistics from social income account of Taiwan agriculture, 1911–1960 (in T$ at 1935–1937 value)*

	(1) Agricultural production per worker		(2) Per capita farm household income		(3) Per capita consumption		(4) Per capita savings		(5) Agricultural investment per worker†		(6)		(7) (8) Agricultural wage rate	
Year	T$	Index	T$	Index	T$	Index	T$	Index	T$	Index	Agricultural population (× 1,000)	Agricultural labor (× 1,000)	T$	Index
1911	156	100	49	100	46	100	2.6	100	8	100	2,106	1,106	0.62	100
1915	148	95	46	95	44	96	2.3	89	6	73	2,240	1,165	0.56	90
1920	172	110	50	103	47	102	2.9	112	10	135	2,279	1,140	0.52	84
1925	238	153	72	148	63	138	8.3	319	24	315	2,322	1,152	0.71	115
1930	258	165	72	148	67	145	5.1	196	23	308	2,512	1,212	0.69	111
1935	289	185	82	170	75	163	7.7	296	12	155	2,746	1,325	0.91	147
1940	290	186	81	168	71	155	10.0	387	31	408	2,955	1,400	0.76	123
1950	278	178	87	180	75	163	12.5	481	35	467	3,939	1,731	0.51	82
1955	327	210	90	185	66	143	24.0	923	60	800	4,546	1,737	0.62	100
1960	385	247	95	195	72	156	23.0	885	66	875	5,174	1,754	0.69	111

Source: Appendix A, "Methods and Sources for Statistical Estimates for Social Income Accounting of Taiwan's Agriculture."

* Estimates for the years 1941–1949 were excluded from consideration, since statistics published by the government during this period were often manipulated or voided for reasons of national security, and because rapid inflation in the postwar period made valuation of commodity and service transactions extremely difficult.

† Refers to fixed capital investment only.

nonagricultural commodities in terms of current price, which correspond with the items 4 and 5 in Table 2 below. The right side of equation (10) corresponds with the gross outflow of funds, item 7, and gross inflow of funds, item 8, and their balance or net outflow of funds, item 9, in the same table.

In equation (11) the left side corresponds with item 13 in the table to indicate the net real capital outflow from the agricultural sector. The right side of equation (12) corresponds with items 11 and 12 in the same table. The first item on the right side indicates the visible net real capital outflow and the second the invisible net real capital outflow, as mentioned above.

The economic meaning of the accounting system with respect to the transformation of agricultural goods to capital goods is made clear as follows. Increase in the production of capital goods generally requires more production resources such as labor and capital goods. And agricultural products contribute to capital formation when they are used as food to feed labor for production of capital goods, a process made evident by the wages–fund theory in classical economics. But the relationship between consumption of food and wage payment has complex exchange problems, and the process of such exchange is possible only through the medium of money. Food, for instance, is the equivalent of money in the exchange economy and is paid for from wages. Since wages are derived from the sale of capital goods, wages should be considered originally as a part of capital goods, but in the form of money. Money, then, is the medium for the transformation of agricultural goods to capital goods in the exchange economy, and, therefore, agricultural surplus should be considered as capital under the guise of money. The transformation of agricultural surplus to capital goods can thus be possible through the workers' increased consumption in the nonagricultural sector, which leads to the production of capital goods. In the case of an open economic system, the direct exchange of agricultural products for capital goods through trade will also be possible. Therefore, transformation of agricultural products to capital goods is feasible through intersectoral and international transactions.

Statistical Measurements, 1895–1960

The statistical results derived from social income accounts of Taiwan's agriculture for the period 1911–1960 are initially expressed at the current price of T$ before 1940 and NT$ after 1950.[4] Converted to constant value with 1935–1937 as the base, total agricultural production increased steadily from T$167 million in 1911 to T$397 million in 1940. In the postwar period, it increased from T$420 million in 1950 to T$676 million in 1960. Total farm family income in 1911 was only T$101 million, and it increased to T$240 million in 1940. After 1950, it increased from T$343 million to T$490 million in a ten-year period. Total agricultural investment was about T$8 million or 8.3 percent of total farm family income in 1911. It increased to T$43 million in 1940, and the proportion of investment to total farm family income increased to 18 percent during this period. In the postwar period, total investment increased from T$60 million in 1950 to T$115 million in 1960, and the proportion of investment of total farm family income increased from 17.6 percent to 23.5 percent. Total consumption and savings of farm household income were, respectively, T$96 million and T$7 million in 1911, increasing respectively to T$209 mil-

---

[4] Appendix A, "Methods and Sources for Statistical Estimates for Social Income Accounting of Taiwan's Agriculture."

lion and T$30 million in 1940. The saving ratio which these amounts of savings represent increased from 5 percent to 12.4 percent. As for the postwar period, consumption and farm saving were T$295 million and T$50 million, respectively, in 1950, and T$370 million and T$118 million in 1960. The saving ratio for the farm sector increased from 14 percent to 24.3 percent during the same period.

During the fifty years from 1911 to 1960, the gross agricultural product per worker at constant 1935–1937 prices, or the average gross labor productivity of agriculture, increased by about 147 percent (Table 1). This corroborates our previous study of agricultural development in Taiwan.[5] Agricultural productivity of labor in Taiwan increased at an annual growth rate of about 1.8 percent in the total period. Column 2 of Table 1 shows the per capita farm household income, indicating changes in the farmers' share of agricultural products and some extra earnings from the nonagricultural sector. As agricultural population increased at a more rapid rate than the agricultural labor force, per capita farm household income increased by only 95 percent or at 1.3 percent per year. Per capita consumption, column 3, increased by 56 percent or at an annual rate of only 0.9 percent. The wage rate in agriculture in 1935–1937 prices was T$0.62 per day in 1911, increased to T$0.91 per day in 1935, and decreased to T$0.69 per day in 1960. During the same period, per capita savings of the agricultural population increased from 100 in 1911 to 885 in 1960 at the rapid annual growth rate of 4.5 percent.

Agricultural investment per worker (column 5) gives an

[5] S. C. Hsieh and T. H. Lee, "Agricultural Development and Its Contributions to Economic Growth in Taiwan," *Economic Digest Series No. 17* (Taipei, Taiwan: Joint Commission on Rural Reconstruction, April 1966), p. 15.

indication of the rise in agricultural labor productivity in Taiwan in the past fifty years. Technological change and increase in per capita investment in agricultural production are the major causes of overall agricultural development in Taiwan. In the period 1930 to 1935, per worker investment declined from T$23 to T$12. Such a rapid decline in per capita investment in this period was due to several reasons which will be examined in Chapter 5.

The above statistics highlight the following specific points:

(a) Net agricultural production increased at an average annual growth rate of 3 percent, and the increase in labor productivity was 1.8 percent per annum through the period 1911–1960. These figures are slightly higher than the 2.67 percent and 1.6 percent of the previous study, which were based on the gross output at 1935–1937 constant price.[6] This rate of growth in agricultural production was much faster than the 1.17 percent of Japan's agriculture in the period of 1877–1960.[7]

(b) Despite the rapid increase in agricultural output and average labor productivity in agriculture, the increase in cultivators' per capita consumption was only 0.9 percent per annum. Two reasons account for this trend of per capita consumption: (1) the increase in agricultural population; and (2) the heavy land rent payment and the farmer's desire for more savings.

(c) High annual growth rate of per capita savings through the whole period is particularly impressive. It shows a close

[6] *Ibid.*, pp. 14, 45.

[7] Kazushi Ohkawa and Bruce F. Johnston, "The Transferability of Japanese Pattern of Modernizing Traditional Agriculture," a paper presented at Conference of the Role of Agriculture in Economic Development at Princeton University, National Bureau of Economic Research, December 1–2, 1967, p. 7.

relationship with per capita investment per worker, except during 1930, and is a positive factor influencing the amount of capital outflow from the agricultural sector.

The sectoral net real capital flow derived with the use of equations (11) and (12) is summarized in Figure 1 and Table 2. The agricultural sector has made a contribution of capital to the nonagricultural sector in Taiwan throughout the period under review. The visible net real capital outflow, or net real agricultural surplus, was increasing before World War II and declining after World War II. When the trend of visible net real capital outflow is compared with sale ratio of agricultural products, both series show a close relationship in the period before 1930 but show no relationship in the periods 1930–1940 and after 1950. In the latter period, the sale ratio was comparatively constant, but visible net real capital outflow fluctuated remarkably.[8] Sale ratio in the period 1950–1960 was lower than that in the prewar period.

Invisible net real capital outflow or inflow can be shown by the difference between net real capital outflow and visible net real capital outflow as illustrated in Figure 1. Except for the years 1925, 1926, 1928, 1929, 1935, and 1936, the invisible net real capital outflow was positive, indicating that the terms of trade were against agriculture, as compared to the base period. As seen in Figure 1, invisible net real capital outflow was particularly large in the postwar period. The terms of trade between the agricultural sector and the nonagricultural sector have shown fluctuations. There is no definite trend through the long period. Roughly speaking, the terms of trade were against agriculture before 1925 and moved toward agriculture in the period 1925–1940. In the

---

[8] For the definition and economic meaning of sale ratio, see Chapter 5.

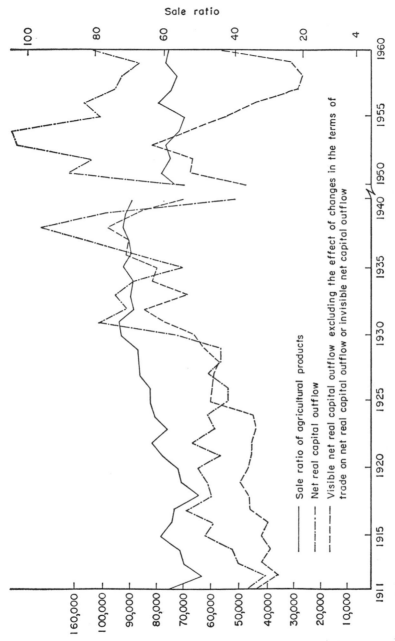

Figure 1. Sale ratio of agricultural products and net real capital outflow, Taiwan, 1911–1960. For the years 1941–1949 see asterisked note, Table 1.

Table 2. Intersectoral capital flows between the agricultural and the nonagricultural sectors, Taiwan, 1895–1960

Item	1895–1900	1901–1905	1906–1910	1911–1915	1916–1920	1921–1925	1926–1930	1931–1935	1936–1940*	1950–1955	1956–1960
1. Total agricultural production (Y_a) T$millions	45†	56†	66†	97	188	243	297	291	508	7,210	16,028
2. Total sale of agricultural products (X) T$millions	—	—	—	55	105	155	204	208	362	4,184	9,665
3. Total sale ratio (X/Y_a) %	—	—	—	56	56	64	69	72	71	58	60
4. Total outflow of agricultural products (X') T$millions	—	—	—	55	105	155	204	208	362	4,184	9,665
a. To nonagricultural production (R^n_a) T$millions	—	—	—	28	56	78	106	88	164	2,013	4,926
b. To nonagricultural household (C^n_a) T$millions	—	—	—	18	30	41	48	48	82	1,942	4,177
c. To foreign countries (E_a) T$millions	—	—	—	9	20	36	51	72	117	229	562
5. Total inflow of nonagricultural products (M) T$millions	—	—	—	31	63	105	143	146	261	3,268	8,716
a. Working capital goods (R^a_n) T$millions	—	—	—	6	17	29	45	47	82	1,053	2,594
b. Fixed capital goods (I_a) T$millions	—	—	—	‡	2	8	11	8	9	107	1,196
c. Consumer goods (C^a_n) T$millions	—	—	—	24	44	68	87	91	169	2,108	4,926
6. Net commodity outflow ($B = X − M$) T$millions	—	—	—	24	42	50	61	63	102	916	948
7. Gross outflow of fund (F) T$millions	15	20	23	29	53	68	76	76	135	1,337	2,616
a. Land rent and interest (Z) T$millions	13§	17§	19§	22	43	52	59	56	98	532	739
b. Taxes and fees (J) T$millions	1‖	3‖	5‖	6	9	15	16	17	30	712	1,453
c. Transfer of fund through financial institutions (Q) T$millions	#	—	—	‡	‡	1	‡	3	6	94	425
8. Gross inflow of fund (G) T$millions	‡	2	2	4	10	18	15	13	33	421	1,668
a. Public investment & subsidy (S) T$millions	‡‖	‡‖	‡‖	2	1	3	4	1	2	26	71
b. Investment by nonagricultural sector in agriculture (H) T$millions	#	—	—	‡	1	3	6	3	5	12	44
c. Income received from the nonagricultural sector (W) T$millions	‡**	‡**	1	2	8	12	5	9	26	383	1,552
9. Net outflow of fund ($B = F − G$) T$millions	14	18	21	24	42	50	61	63	102	916	948
10. Terms of trade ($T = P_n/P_a$) %	—	—	—	121	130	112	100	107	102	126	120
a. Agricultural price index (P_a: 1935–1937 = 100) %	—	—	—	60	92	102	103	80	120	1,405	2,484
b. Nonagricultural price index (P_n: 1935–1937 = 100) %	—	—	—	73	119	114	103	86	123	1,766	2,975

11. Visible net real capital outflow ($V_1 = B/P_a$)
    T$millions at 1935–1937 price

—	—	—	41	46	49	59	78	85	65	38

12. Invisible net real capital outflow
    [$V_2 = M/P_n (T - 1)$] T$mil. at 1935–1937 price

—	—	—	9	16	11	(−)‡	11	5	48	58

13. Net real capital outflow ($B' = X/P_a - M/P_n$)
    T$millions at 1935–37 price

14	18	21	50	62	60	59	89	90	113	96

14. X/P_a T$millions at 1935–1937 price

—	—	—	92	116	152	198	259	302	298	389

15. M/P_n T$millions at 1935–1937 price

—	—	—	42	53	92	140	170	212	185	293

Source: Appendix A.

* For the years 1941–1949 see asterisked note, Table 1.

† Total agricultural production value from 1902–1910 was quoted from "Taiwan Agricultural Statistics," annual issue. The data prior to 1902 were estimated by using the growth rates of total cultivated land area and of agricultural population. Per capita agricultural production in unit land area (hectare) in 1902 was used as the basis to extrapolate back each year's agricultural population and cultivated land area.

‡ Under 1 million.

§ For estimate of land rent and interest in each year the ratios of land rent and interest to total agricultural production were used. A ratio of 20 percent was used for the period 1904–1910 after land-reform program and of 31 percent for the period 1895–1903.

‖ Taxes, government subsidy, and investment were quoted from "The Reports of Government Budget," annual issue.

The figures for agricultural loans and saving deposits in financial institutions were not available for 1895–1918, since no financial institutions existed in rural areas in this period.

** Estimate of nonfarm income received by farmers was based on the ratio between nonfarm income and the value of industrial production. Value of industrial production was 43.9 million T$ and nonfarm income was 2.6 million T$ in 1911, producing a ratio of 5.8. The source of the data is "The Commercial and Manufacturing Statistics," Taiwan Governor General's Office, annual issue.

postwar period, they were most unfavorable to agriculture.

From the systematic accounting of net real capital flows between sectors as shown in Table 2, it is useful to compare our definition with other definitions of the sectoral capital flows. Item 7c in the table indicates the fund outflow through financial institutions which is generally called gross savings in agriculture. The amount of net savings in agriculture can be obtained by deducting item 8a, public investment and subsidy, and item 8b, investment in agriculture by the non-agricultural sector, from the gross savings in agriculture. This terminology is commonly used in the literature on agricultural development. It is apparent that the amount of net savings in agriculture is far less than the amount of net outflow of funds (B) in equation (9) above, and they each show a different trend through the total period. As we mentioned before, the term net savings in agriculture is not appropriate for sectoral capital outflow.

One may consider an inflow of funds into agriculture as that consisting of payments for labor, capital, and property services of the agricultural sector to the nonagricultural sector, while those funds which flow out from the agricultural sector for payment of land rent and interest to the nonagricultural sector constitute an outflow from the agricultural sector. The difference between the two items is defined as the net outflow or inflow of capital through the current account of funds. The most probable objection to this accounting is that these items should not be included in the accounting of sectoral capital flow. If this is correct, balance of social income account and change in national capital accounts will not correspond with each other, and a systematic accounting of the sectoral capital flow will be impossible. Because the payment of the factor services between sectors is an important component of the sectoral income stream and the balance is the financial claim of one sector against another sector, this is also the source of capital contribution of one sector to another sector. Objections to our accounting procedure presumably stem from misconceptions about capital, a matter which will be discussed in Chapter 6.

The total real agricultural surplus (TAS) is also an important conventional scale for measuring sectoral capital outflows. In Table 2, item 14 shows the real total sale of agricultural products (TAS) to the nonagricultural sector. The amount of this item is larger than net commodity or net fund outflow and also larger than visible and invisible net real capital outflow. When we compare the trend of total real outflow of agricultural products with that of the net real capital outflow, we cannot find a relationship between the two series. This means also that the total real outflow of agricultural products (TAS) is not a good indicator of net real capital contribution of the agricultural sector.

From the above discussion, it is clear that different statistical scales derived from different conventional concepts of the sectoral capital flows show different magnitudes of capital contribution and different trends of change. Net real capital outflow in item 13, which is derived on the basis of a rigorous definition and systematic accounting of capital, can be considered the most inclusive and appropriate scale for measuring sectoral capital outflow from agriculture. Therefore, we will attempt to identify the important components of the net real capital outflow in Taiwan's agricultural development.

The factors determining the net real capital outflow are net real agricultural surplus, or visible net real capital outflow, and changes in terms of trade. Net real agricultural surplus has a close relationship with the increase in real agricultural production, a relationship which is dependent on changes in the sale ratio of agricultural products. The sale ratio, as shown in Figure 1, had three different phases: it increased in the period 1911–1930, it was stable at a higher level during 1930–1940, and it was unstable at a lower level in the postwar period 1950–1960. Net agricultural surplus has shown a correspondingly different relationship with fluctuations in agricultural production. Figure 2 indicates the relationship between changes in real agricultural production and in net real agricultural surplus, and here the net real agricultural surplus annual changes are shown to be quite regular in the period 1911–1930. The increasing trend in the sale ratio and the comparatively stable increase in real agricultural production are important relevant factors. In the period 1930–1940, the net real agricultural surplus showed great fluctuations since the sale ratio was stable while real agricultural production was not. In the period 1950–1960, the sale ratio declined while agricultural production fluctuated greatly. It can be said, therefore, that net real agricultural surplus changed irregularly.

In the total sale of agricultural products during the whole period, sale of agricultural raw materials constituted more than half the share as seen in Table 2. Sale to nonagricultural households was about 33 percent of the total sales of agricultural products during 1911–1915, but decreased to about 23 percent during 1935–1940. It increased again to 43 percent in 1956–1960. Percentage of direct agricultural exports in the total sale of agricultural products was about 16 percent in 1911–1915, increasing to 32 percent in 1936–1940, and then decreasing to 5.8 percent in 1956–1960. These facts show that composite factors of total sale or demand for agricultural products in Taiwan have varied in their importance in accordance with changes in population growth, level of people's income, foreign market conditions, and develop-

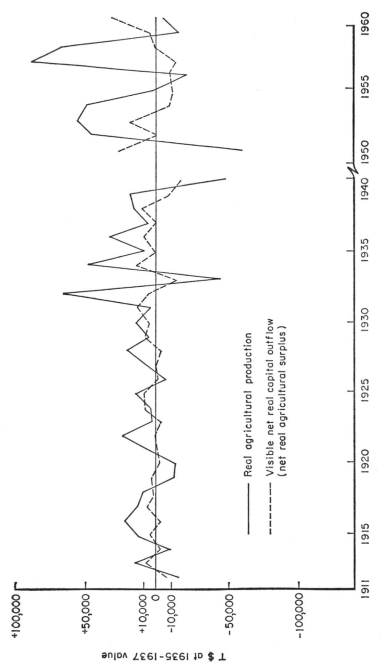

Figure 2. The first differences of real agricultural production and net real agricultural surplus (or visible net real capital outflow), Taiwan, 1911–1960. For the years 1941–1949 see asterisked note, Table 1.

ment of domestic industry. Through the whole period, a small portion of agricultural surplus was consumed by the nonagricultural household sector, but it has become more important in the postwar period. Further analysis of this point will be made in Chapter 5.

Of the total inflow of nonagricultural products, consumer goods accounted for 79 percent in 1911–1915, but declined to 65 percent in 1936–1940. In the postwar period, consumer goods made up 65 percent of the inflow in 1950–1955 and 57 percent in 1956–1960. These proportions coincide with the slow increase in per capita consumption as shown in Table 1.

Working capital goods for agricultural production, including chemical fertilizer, feed, chemicals, and farm implements and tools, were only 19 percent of total inflow of nonagricultural products in 1911–1915. This figure increased rapidly to 32 percent in 1936–1940 and declined to 30 percent in 1956–1960. Consumption in agriculture of fixed capital goods which flowed from the nonagricultural sector was only 2 percent of total inflow of nonagricultural goods in 1911–1915, increasing to 6 percent in 1931–1935, and declining until the midfifties. In the postwar period, this consumption increased from 3 percent in 1950–1955 to 14 percent in 1956–1960. Demand in the agricultural sector for nonagricultural goods was determined by a mix of the above factors, in which demand for consumer goods was large in the initial period and demand for working capital goods and fixed capital goods became larger in the later period of agricultural development. In particular, demand for fixed capital goods significantly increased in the period 1956–1960, but its total amount was still small compared with other items.

Gross outflow of funds includes such items as: (a) land rent paid to the resident and absentee landlords and interest paid to financial institutions and money lenders; (b) government taxing and donations, and fees paid to irrigation associations and farmers' associations; and (c) net savings deposited and invested in nonagricultural sector through financial institutions. In the period 1911–1915, land rent and interest comprised 78 percent of the gross outflow of funds. This figure declined to about 73 percent in 1936–1940. After land reform in the postwar period, it was only 28 percent of total gross outflow of funds. Taxes and fees in the prewar period remained at 17 to 22 percent of gross outflow of funds. This amount increased to 53 percent in 1950–1955 and to 56 percent in 1956–1960. The above items, (a) and (b), are generally considered as entries in the current account. Item (c) is an entry in the capital account. The autonomous flow of capital funds was a very limited amount in the beginning and increased to 16 percent in the period 1956–1960. We will discuss these points in more detail in Chapter 6.

Gross inflow of funds includes (a) public investment and subsidy, (b) investment in the agricultural sector made by landlords, and long-term loans from financial institutions, (c) farmers' receipts from nonfarm income. Public investment and subsidy to agriculture exceeded 38 percent of total gross inflow of funds in the initial period and declined to below 5 percent in 1956–1960. Conversely, nonfarm income increased steadily from 54 percent of total gross inflow of funds in 1911–1915 to 93 percent in 1956–1960. Investments made by absentee landlords and long-term loans from financial institutions also increased from 7 percent in 1911–1915 to 16 percent in 1936–1940 before declining sharply in the postwar period. Land reform programs and limited amounts of long-term funds for agriculture contributed to this decrease in the postwar period.

In order to analyze the impact of net real capital outflow

on economic development as a whole, we must view statistics for several composite factors. For this purpose, estimates of national income, total capital formation, wage rates in two sectors, export and import surpluses, indices of industrial production, share of labor income, labor productivity, and government receipts and expenditures are presented in Table 3. Here it is shown that the net domestic product of Taiwan has increased at an average rate of 3.0 percent for the period 1911–1960. Although the growth rate annually averaged 4.1 percent in the prewar period from 1911–1915 to 1936–1940, it was 8.0 percent in the period from 1951– 1955 to 1956–1960. Such fast growth of the national economy was largely due to rapid accumulation of capital. Capital accumulation in the total national economy increased at a rate of 4.3 percent annually in the prewar period from 1911–1915 to 1936–1940 and at a rate of 8.0 percent annually in the period from 1951–1955 to 1956–1960. The growth rates of national income and capital accumulation were roughly the same through the entire period, indicating an approximately constant capital-output ratio. Net real capital outflow from agriculture increased at a rate of 3.8 percent annually in the prewar period from 1911–1915 to 1936–1940 and at an annual rate of 10 percent in the period from 1951–1955 to 1956– 1960, as shown in Table 2. The increase in export surplus in the prewar period and its decrease in the postwar period indicate the variety of ways in which the net real capital outflow from agriculture contributed to the national economy. Under the Japanese colonial system, though an inflow of private capital and government financing from Japan had occurred, the amount of capital transfer from Taiwan to Japan through export surplus was still remarkable. This implies that Taiwan's agriculture had contributed not only to the individual development in Taiwan, but also to the

Table 3. Economic indicators of the impact of net real capital outflow from agriculture on economic development, Taiwan, 1911–1960 (in T$ at 1935–1937 value)

Items	1911–1915	1916–1920	1921–1925	1926–1930	1931–1935	1936–1940*	1951–1955	1956–1960
Net domestic product at factor cost (T$million)	294	337	399	560	706	797	795	1,119
Capital formation (T$million)	29†	31	35	52	76	89	151	242
Exports (T$million)	106	143	177	249	315	377	74	128
Imports (T$million)	95	102	118	184	224	288	76	130
Export surplus (T$million)	11	41	60	65	91	90	Δ2‡	Δ2‡
Industrial prod. index (% with 1935–1937 base)	18†	32	41	64	82	116	95	159
Labor productivity of industry (T$)	569	828	676	867	1,031	1,091	807	1,089
Labor force in industry (1,000 persons)	138	153	162	172	203	247	273	341
Total population (1,000 persons)	3,486	3,677	3,981	4,449	5,061	5,756	8,452	10,069
Percent of domestic food consumption in production (%)	84	80	77	72	62	58	94	95
Share of labor income in industry (%)	47	36	42	37	36	21	41	36
General price index (% with 1935–1937 base)	62	112	116	102	87	133	2,202	3,423
Wage rate in industry (T$ per day)	0.71	0.90	0.74	0.86	0.99	0.60	0.74	0.77
Net real capital outflow (T$million)	50	62	60	59	89	90	113	96
Visible net real outflow (T$million)	41	46	49	59	78	85	65	38
Invisible net real outflow (T$million)	9	16	11	§	11	5	48	58

Source: Appendix A.

* For years 1941–1950, see asterisked note, Table 1.

† The 1911 total is not available; this figure is based on 1912–1915.

‡ Δ = import surplus.

§ Under 1 million.

industrial development in Japan. In the postwar period, as we will analyze it in detail later, the contribution of real visible capital flow from agriculture to total capital formation was not large, but the real invisible capital outflow was large. The squeeze on agriculture through the policy of low agricultural prices was obviously effective. We will devote our efforts in the following chapters to the analysis of this phenomenon.

Industrial production increased quite rapidly through the whole period from 1911 to 1960. Of the total industrial products, agricultural processing products represented about 60 to 80 percent during the whole period. Increase in the sale of agricultural products to the nonagricultural sector would be a direct contribution of agriculture to industries. Sale of agricultural products to nonfarm households and invisible outflow of real capital would benefit industrialists and industrial workers by supplying cheap sources of raw materials and wages. The contribution of the agricultural sector in this respect was particularly significant in the early period of the prewar stage and in the entire postwar period. Despite small increases in the wage rate, the share of labor income declined during the whole period, 1911–1960. The important fact is that the wage rate has not increased greatly in proportion to the increase in labor productivity in industry.

Increase in the labor force of industry lagged far behind the increase in total population. Despite this fact, domestic food consumption as percent of total food production declined from 84 percent in 1911–1915 to 58 percent in 1936–1940 and climbed to 94 percent in the postwar period. The general price level was maintained with only a slight increase in the prewar period compared with the rapid inflationary trend of the postwar period. This price level will be discussed in detail after analyzing the effect of net real capital transfer from agriculture on economic growth and development of international trade.

The above statistical findings are based on estimates of the various important economic indicators of the net real capital outflow from the agricultural sector in Taiwan. The problems suggested above will need further analysis in the following chapters, and the issues to be considered are: (a) the processes and patterns of increasing agricultural production; and (b) the financial and physical processes of transferring net real capital from agriculture.

 CHAPTER 3

Agricultural
Development Policy

From a study of the statistical findings set forth in Chapter 2, we know that there was a net real capital outflow from agriculture through the entire period 1911–1960, that it had an increasing trend, and that it fluctuated from period to period. The trend and fluctuation of net real capital outflow from agriculture are strongly influenced by the level of agricultural production and the means used to obtain the outflow. These two factors are in turn importantly influenced by the initial conditions of agricultural development and by the nature of development goals and policies. In addition, if lessons are to be drawn for application to the South Asian countries, it is important to know to what extent conditions in Taiwan at initiation of its development were similar to current conditions in South Asian countries and what the policies were which achieved the particular pattern of development.

Conditions in Agriculture before 1895

When Taiwan was ceded to Japan in 1895, it is estimated to have had a population of 2.6 million and 550 thousand hectares of cultivated land. Irrigation facilities were limited, and the land was farmed with traditional methods.[1] Develop-

[1] The total population and cultivated land area in 1895 were estimated by the author by extrapolating the rates of population growth and cultivated land in 1905–1915. See details in the following sections.

ment of farming skills, crop patterns, and rice yields for the period before 1895 can be quickly summarized from the limited records available.

The first agricultural practices were brought to Taiwan by Chinese immigrants from mainland China around 1600. Large-scale immigration began only after 1624 during the period of Dutch control of the island. At this time shortage of labor and of animal power was the most limiting factor in the expansion of agricultural production. In order to increase its revenue from taxes on land and customs duties, the East India Company encouraged Chinese immigration and also imported cattle for land reclamation and farming. The important crops then included rice, sugarcane, beans, and vegetables. The average per hectare yield of rice was about 8.74 Koku, which is equivalent to 1.0 M/T of brown rice.[2]

More skillful farming practices, particularly in rice cultivation, were brought in after the Ching occupation in 1683. The large immigration with its introduction of new farming skills from South China maintained a rice yield of 1.3 M/T per hectare until 1895, although the land gradually became less fertile. Okuda reports that, without the use of fertilizers, soil fertility usually decreased after two or three years of cultivation. Farmers then shifted to new land.[3] In the following two hundred years farming practices became more advanced. Organic fertilizers were applied as the soil lost its fertility, and new land became increasingly scarce. Small irrigation facilities and catchment ponds were constructed to supply water for rice cultivation in the dry season.

[2] Iku Okuda et al., "Oranda jidai Taiwan nōgyō" (in Japanese) [Taiwan's Agriculture in the Dutch Period], in T'aiwan ching-chi shih tsu-chi (in Chinese) [Series of Taiwan Economic History No. 1] (Taipei, Taiwan: Bank of Taiwan, 1954), pp. 45–47. Koku = 1.45 kg.

[3] Okuda, ibid.

Changing the rice variety from year to year was one method which prevented degeneration of the crop; improved seeds in the modern sense did not exist. In 1895, there were 1,679 varieties of rice, all of indica type.[4]

In the nineteenth century land pressure was still less in Taiwan than in mainland China, but the problems of disease, typhoon, and drought were great. The land-man ratio in this period, as described by Okuda, was estimated at 2 to 3 hectares per family.[5] This is quite similar to the present situation in South Asian countries. Factor proportions of labor and land might have changed gradually through the decrease in farm land area per family, but technological change was so slow that productivity of labor barely increased during two hundred years. Under the great threat of natural hazards, especially typhoon and insects, and in conditions of social instability in the initial period of Taiwan settlement, agriculture prior to 1895 was presumably in a state of primitive stagnation, or of cyclical movement of slow progress and regression through two centuries.

LEVEL OF PER CAPITA INCOME AND INCOME ORIGINATING IN AGRICULTURE

The net national product of Taiwan in constant prices has been estimated by the author over the period of 1911–1940. From the estimated rates of growth in per capita national product and agricultural production at 1911–1915 prices, we have, for our purposes, extrapolated back to a figure of about US$25 as the per capita income in 1895, expressed in 1935–1937 prices. To make it comparable to per capita income levels derived by Kuznets for developing

[4] Shigeto Kawano, *Taiwan beikoku keizai don* (in Japanese) [Rice Economy of Taiwan] (Tokyo: Yuhikaku, 1941), pp. 16–17 (hereafter referred to as *Rice Economy of Taiwan*).

[5] Okuda, "Taiwan's Agriculture in the Dutch Period," *op. cit.*, p. 47.

countries, the 1935–1937 dollar value has been converted to 1949 U.S. dollar value which raises it to US$46 for 1895. This was less than one-third of per capita income of developed countries at their initial period of industrialization between 1840 and 1850.[6] The figure is similar to the per capita incomes of Korea, Thailand, Burma, Yeman, Saudi Arabia, Ecuador, and Haiti, and less than that of Philippines, Pakistan and India in 1949.[7]

Viewing the distribution of national income in industries in the period 1911–1915, primary industries including agriculture, fisheries, forestry, and mining accounted for about 48 percent of the total income, and secondary and tertiary industries respectively accounted for 27 percent and 25 percent.[8] It seems likely that in 1895 about 65 to 70 percent of the national income originated in primary industries, largely in agricultural production. There is no doubt that agriculture was the main source of national income, and low per capita income in this period was due mainly to the primitive methods of production in agriculture.

POPULATION AND THE MAN-LAND RATIO

Population and labor force data are not available for 1895. On the basis of average growth rates in the period 1905–1915,[9] population and labor force in 1895 are estimated at

[6] Simon Kuznets, "Underdeveloped Countries and the Pre-Industrial Phase in the Advanced Countries," *The Economics of Underdevelopment,* ed. A. N. Agurwala, *et al.* (Oxford: Oxford University Press, 1958), pp. 135–136.

[7] Kuznets, *ibid.,* p. 136.

[8] National income statistics for the period 1911–1940 were estimated by the author. See Hsieh and Lee, "Agricultural Development and Its Contributions to Economic Growth in Taiwan," *op. cit.,* Appendix Table 1.

[9] George W. Barclay, *Colonial Development and Population in Taiwan* (Princeton, New Jersey: Princeton University Press, 1954), pp. 146–147.

2.6 million and 1.3 million.[10] By similar procedures, agricultural population and labor force in 1895 were estimated to be approximately 1.8 million and 1.0 million. The proportion of agricultural population and labor force in total population and total labor force would respectively be about 65 to 70 percent and 75 to 80 percent in 1895. The average number of persons per farm family was about 5.8 in 1902.[11] Based on the above estimate of agricultural population, the total number of farm families would be estimated as 305,000 in 1895 with the assumption of 5.8 persons per farm family. The official report of cultivated land area for 1895 is considered an underestimate because of nonreporting (largely to avoid taxes). The new estimate of total cultivated land area for 1895 stands at 550 thousand hectares.[12] On the basis of these estimates, the average farm size would have been around 1.8 hectares in 1895. This estimate seems consistent with other data on farmers' living standards, average size of farm families, crop yields, and crop production patterns.

With the slow increase in the number of irrigation facili-

[10] The population growth rate of 13 percent for the ten years from 1895–1905 was adopted for this estimate. The difference between the Chinese who left and the Japanese who came in during this period is assumed to be 50,000.

[11] Taiwan Governor General's Office, *Taiwan nōgyō nen-pō* [Taiwan Agricultural Yearbook], published in Japanese from 1901–1940 and in Chinese with a title *T'aiwan Nung-yeh nien-pao* from 1945–1960 (Taipei, Taiwan, 1902), pp. 24–25 (hereafter referred to as *Taiwan Agricultural Yearbook*).

[12] For the estimate, the average annual increase in cultivated land area was assumed to be 7,700 hectares. This figure reflects the fact that land reclamation in this period was done by human and animal labor only, and that about 200 man days and 100 animal days were required for reclaiming one hectare of land. Considering the total number of population and labor force in agriculture and their regular farming days per worker per year, the maximum possible expansion of cultivated land area was estimated as 7,700 hectares in a year.

ties in the period 1895–1903, the share of paddy and dry land stood at 45 percent and 55 percent respectively. The multiple cropping index was estimated to be 110 or 605,000 hectares of crop area based on the rate of increase in crop area recorded later. Per capita cultivated land and cropland areas in terms of agricultural labor (estimated as 1,006,000 in 1895) were 0.55 and 0.60 hectare respectively. Comparing these statistics with the present South Asian countries, the land-man ratio in this early period of Taiwan history was far less than in most of these countries.

Irrigated land area was officially reported to have been 107,716 hectares in 1895.[13] Although an irrigation survey was conducted in 1900, and the Public Irrigation Law was passed in 1901, no new irrigation projects were initiated and only repair jobs were conducted before 1903. Thus, the figure of 180,000 hectares for 1900 is probably a more reliable indication of irrigated land area in 1895. This was roughly 32 percent of total cultivated land area, higher than that now current in most South Asian countries.[14]

CROP YIELDS AND LAND PRODUCTIVITY

The estimate of yields of major crops for 1895 is based on official reports of 1900–1905. The yield of rice averaged 1.3 M/T per hectare in the period 1901–1905, and, although the rice improvement program was not started by the Japanese until 1905, it is conceivable that the yield of rice had already achieved the level of 1.3 M/T per hectare in 1895. The sugar-

[13] *Taiwan Agricultural Yearbook*, 1900 ed., p. 21.
[14] Ishikawa, *Economic Development in Asian Perspective*, pp. 106–107. The proportions of irrigated land in the South Asian countries have been reported as: Burma 3.86% (1962), Ceylon 9.37% (1963), Malaya 9.08% (1963), India 15.23% (1961), Philippines 9.37% (1959), and Thailand 17.15% (1962).

Table 4. Agricultural net output per hectare
in South Asian countries in 1960
and in Taiwan in 1895

Country	Agricultural net output per hectare (U.S.$ in 1960)	Yield of rice M/T/ha.
Taiwan (1895)	103	1.30
India (1960)	91	1.36
Pakistan (1960)	133	1.45
Thailand ((1960)	106	1.37
Philippines (1960)	139	1.17

Source: United States Department of Agriculture, *Changes in Agriculture in 26 Developing Countries* (Foreign Agricultural Economic Report No. 27, 1963), p. 89. The statistics of agricultural net output per hectare for other countries were compiled from the average agricultural output in 1958–1960.

cane improvement program started earlier than the rice program, and new sugarcane varieties were introduced from the Hawaiian Islands in 1896. The original variety of sugarcane grown in Taiwan was the small type of bamboo cane, and it yielded only 20 M/T per hectare and contained only 7.5 percent of sugar. The yield of sweet potatoes in 1895 is estimated at about 5.0 M/T per hectare based on the trend for the period 1900–1910. The peanut yield was estimated at 0.5 M/T per hectare in 1895 by the same method as that used for sweet potatoes.

Using the given weights of prices for the above major crops and assuming constant yields for minor crops, the combined aggregate crop yield index thus obtained was only 85 percent in 1895 using 1911–1915 as the base. In a long series, the crop yield index for 1895 is 51.6 percent of the 1935–1937 base.

Crop yield and the multiple cropping index have a combined effect on output per hectare or average land productivity. The average net output per hectare in 1895 was estimated with an assumption of constant crop patterns at only T\$155 or US\$46 per hectare in 1935–1937 dollars or US\$103 in 1960 dollars.

As seen in Table 4, the average land productivity in Taiwan in 1895 is comparable with that of the South Asian countries in 1960.

Agricultural Development Policy in Taiwan

Growth of the agricultural sector in Taiwan was closely related to that of other sectors, particularly since the government generally was prepared to intervene in the intersectoral relationships to arrange for allocating capital among different sectors. The government's role in increasing agricultural production with a special emphasis on the intersectoral capital flows will be discussed.

INITIAL PHASE OF DEVELOPMENT

The first phase covers the period 1895–1930, which represents early Japanese colonialism. It was a period of learning, designing, and construction in Taiwan. The initial problem facing the colonial government in shaping a program was to survey, inventory, and register the resources. The important guiding principle in selecting the alternative programs in Taiwan was to supplement the needs of the Japanese Empire. These included, first, an early termination of subsidies from the Japanese treasury, and second, an increase of sugar and rice production so as to meet the domestic requirements and to make up the foreign exchange deficit.

Development programs emphasized both material input as well as institutional organization. Emphasis was placed on heavy investment in infrastructure, such as communications, transportation, harbors, power, education, general public health, flood control, and irrigation, especially for agriculture. Institutional and organizational reforms were imposed on the administrative system, land tenure system, monetary and financial system, and farmers' associations. Government expenditure for the above investment largely came from Japanese treasury subsidies and government debt issues until 1904 when the Taiwanese government became self-financing through increased profit from government monopolies, a consumption tax on sugar, and an increase in the land tax.

Chang and Myers list the following reasons for such rapid achievement of Taiwan's financial independence from Japan: (a) a policy of deficit financing adopted in 1898; (b) the introduction of new taxes and the raising of old taxes after a rapidly executed land survey and an increase in sugar production; (c) the administration's establishment of a monopoly on the sale of salt, opium, tobacco, and camphor.[15] As will be discussed in the following chapter, the development financing in Taiwan was different from that of the Meiji government in Japan which had relied heavily on the single item of land tax.

Agricultural development in this period concentrated mainly on sugarcane and rice. Agricultural experiment stations were established, initially to make simple indigenous improvements in technology and plant varieties. In conjunction with this indigenous effort, specialists were brought in to engage in more extensive research in agricultural technology, as a result of which 300 Indica rice varieties, out of the 1,679 varieties grown in Taiwan, were retained, and new

[15] Han-yi Chang and Ramon H. Myers, "Japanese Colonial Development Policy in Taiwan, 1895–1906: A Case Study of Bureaucratic Entrepreneurship," *Journal of Asian Studies,* XXII, No. 4 (August 1963), 448.

sugarcane varieties such as Rose Bamboo and Lohaina were adopted from the Hawaiian Islands. Beginning in 1902 application of chemical fertilizers was encouraged for sugarcane production at first with a subsidy. Production of green manure and compost was introduced to the rice growing farmers.

Irrigation came under government control in 1901. Before that date, irrigation projects had consisted largely of repairing damaged canals, but now expansion of paddy land and protection from the hazard of drought were the main goals of the program. Institutional roles underwent significant changes in this period with the creation of the landlord class, the leaders of the Pao-chia system. They were convinced that agricultural improvement was to their benefit under the new land-tenure system and land-tax payment. They were encouraged to direct villagers to adopt new seed varieties and better cultivation methods. Kawano indicates that extension of new agricultural technology in Taiwan was very cheap in terms of government expenditure and crop production costs.[16] The farmers' positive response to new technology, in this period, was pervasive, largely because of the influence of the landlord class and the government.

The profitability of the new technology, however, was not broadly recognized by cultivators until 1922, when the new variety of Pon-lai rice appeared and previous investment in agriculture began to show results.[17] The process of altering the old cultivation methods and the extension of use of the new varieties in this period was not characterized by persuasion, but rather by government enforcement. Police stayed in the local communities and effectively participated in agri-

[16] Kawano, *Rice Economy of Taiwan,* pp. 57–58.
[17] *Ibid.,* pp. 59–65.

cultural extension services.[18] The period 1895–1930 is characterized by economic and social development measures which provided a solid basis for later growth.

RAPID DEVELOPMENT OF AGRICULTURE AND THE START OF INDUSTRIALIZATION

The years 1931–1940 were characterized by technological achievement and economic persuasion of farmers. For the period under review, agricultural development was second only to that of the postwar period of recovery and rehabilitation from 1945 to 1952.

Following the measures undertaken in the period 1895–1930 for shaping and constructing economic and social overhead and institutional organization, further efforts were made by the colonial government to promote agricultural development through institutional and technological improvements. The guiding principle of the government was maximum utilization of the invested capital to achieve profitable production. Implementation by government shifted from police enforcement to persuasion through proof of the profitability of improved technology. The people's participation and financial support were considered indispensable to development programs in the period. Consequently, many kinds of new agricultural institutions were established in the period 1920–1930, including farmers' cooperatives, landlord-tenant associations, irrigation associations, agricultural improvement groups, and reorganized farmers' associations. The rapid expansion of the Japanese economy in the 1920's and the subsequent recession in the 1930's forced Taiwan

[18] Shungi Shihomi, "Keisatsu to keizai" (translated into Chinese) [Police and Economy], in T'aiwan ching-chi shih tsu-chi (in Chinese) [Series of Taiwan Economic History No. 1] (Taipei, Taiwan: Bank of Taiwan, 1954), pp. 127–147.

to manage its agricultural production by more efficient methods. But the comparatively high prices of rice and sugar in the Japanese market also provided an incentive to farmers to increase their production. The regulation of rice exports announced in 1932 was intended to maintain the price of rice in the Japanese market. The main purpose of regulation was to support the farm income of Japanese farmers through price stabilization. For Taiwan's agriculture, this was an opportunity to adjust the production to largely domestic consumption and to start industrialization on the Island. Diversification and rotational cropping patterns became prominent farming practices.

As a result of increased agricultural output and productivity in this period, both land rents and land prices went up sharply. These were retarding factors to economic transformation and further agricultural development. The adjustment of land rent to safeguard the interest of cultivators was publicly urged.

PERIODS OF RECOVERY AND FURTHER GROWTH

Taiwan was restored to China and placed under a different administration system after World War II. Its economy was in disorder at the beginning of the postwar period. Inflation threatened living costs, and food shortages were aggravated by the large influx of migrants from the Chinese mainland. In 1945–1950 the price index of food averaged 40 percent higher than the general price index. This situation, however, did not last long. With favorable prices of farm products, and continued supply of production goods, particularly of chemical fertilizer from United Nations Relief and Rehabilitation Administration (UNRRA), agricultural production revived gradually and steadily.

Aside from the partial recovery of the technical level of

production and the reorganization of farmers' associations, the most significant of all agricultural undertakings in the period was the land-rent reduction program started in 1949. Emergence of a strong government with the power to push its objective of economic advancement and with the professional competence to carry out its programs was crucial in instituting improved and adequate organizations for development. As a first step toward land reform this program produced dramatic results in providing a basis for more intensive use of both human and land resources through application of modern farming techniques and adjustment of farm organization and operation.

The index of agricultural prices maintained an average of 70 percent of the general price index at the 1935–1937 base in the period 1950–1960. The increase of agricultural production was due in substantial part to the enthusiasm for work and incentive for higher incomes generated among farmers by the land-reform program.[19] The four-year agricultural development plans provided an additional boost to production. The first four-year plan started in 1953 and was followed by a second and a third, ending in 1964. Under the plans, emphasis was placed on developing water resources, marginal slope lands, and forest and fishery resources in coordination with the United States aid program. Technological improvement was simultaneously achieved by adopting a more intensive and coordinated approach. Capital funds were allocated to different development projects according to the required growth rates, and farmers were given guid-

---

[19] H. S. Tang and S. C. Hsieh, "Land Reform and Agricultural Development in Taiwan," *The Malayan Economic Review,* Vol. VI, No. 1 (April 1961), 49–54.

ance and assistance in developing and carrying out their own production plans.[20]

The postwar advance of agricultural technology has been remarkable. Following the technical progress made in the prewar period, new and improved methods have been continuously developed and put into practice. Small farmers have made effective use of the new chemicals, fertilizers, and other production goods as they became increasingly available. Advances in agricultural technology in this period have consisted mainly of extension of the utilization of fertilizer and compost, new pesticides, new crop varieties of rice, and many improved cultivation practices. As a result of these efforts, considerable gains have been made in boosting per hectare yield and in increasing the index of multiple cropping with a better crop-rotation system.

The livestock improvement programs initiated in this period included establishment of prefectural veterinary diagnostic centers, mass vaccination of hogs and other livestock, programs of hybrid hog production, promotion of dairy farming, and use of artificial insemination.

Changes in people's consumption patterns have had a noticeable effect on diversification of farming, as indicated by the rapid growth rates in the production of livestock, fisheries, and special crops. As land resources could be expanded only to a limited extent in this last period, a shift from crops to other items in agricultural production was necessary. Among the new developments were mushroom culture, dairy farming, and handicraft production. The pres-

[20] S. C. Hsieh and T. H. Lee, "An Analytical Review of Agricultural Development in Taiwan—An Input-Output and Productivity Approach," *Economic Digest Series No. 12* (Taipei, Taiwan: Joint Commission on Rural Reconstruction; July 1958), pp. 49–52.

sure of the population explosion and underemployment in rural areas called for intensification of the efforts of labor and capital in order to further expansion of land resources and land capacity.

United States aid, administered through the Joint Commission on Rural Reconstruction, played an important role in this last period. Between 1950 and 1962, the Joint Commission on Rural Reconstruction spent NT$3,000 million on 5,727 projects covering a wide range of activities; its contribution provided 35 percent of the total agricultural capital investment.[21]

This survey of the Taiwanese agriculture over a period of sixty-five years clearly indicates evolvement of the program for rural reconstruction. At the initial stage, the level of development as reflected in the per capita income, yields per hectare, and man-land ratio in Taiwan, was quite comparable to that of the South Asian countries in 1960. In the development process, the government of Taiwan played a positive role: its contribution in the initial stages consisted mainly of creation of infrastructure and institutional framework and, in the later period, of promotion and extension of technology. At no time did the policies emphasize one feature of the developmental process at the expense of another. Indeed, the measures adopted at various times were carefully devised to meet the requirements of the argicultural sector in that specific stage.

[21] "An Estimate of Agricultural Capital Formation in Taiwan, 1955–1961," unpublished report (Taipei, Taiwan: Joint Commission on Rural Reconstruction), Tables 1–3.

CHAPTER 4

Process and Pattern of Growth
in Agricultural Production

The statistical data derived in Chapter 2 suggest that increase in agricultural production and in the sale ratio of agricultural products are most important in increasing the net real agricultural surplus or visible real capital outflow from the agricultural sector. In the case of agricultural development in Taiwan, there has been a net real agricultural surplus throughout the period 1895–1960. In this chapter, we will analyze the process by which that increase in agricultural production was achieved.

Growth of Population, Labor Force, and Labor Productivity

Population growth has an important influence on the choice and progress of resource use and technological change in agriculture. Taiwan has been particularly subject to sharp changes in population growth. Population in Taiwan increased from about 2.6 million in 1895 to 10.0 million in 1960, or about fourfold in sixty-five years. Although the average growth rate for the whole period was 2.10 percent per year, the growth rate was much faster at the end than at the beginning. A rapid decrease in the crude death rate was mainly responsible for an accelerated population increase in the later periods. Immigration was particularly rapid in the two periods 1895–1910 and 1946–1950.

The population growth pattern can be generally classified

into the following four periods: (a) growth rate at low level in 1896–1925; (b) trend toward increasing growth rate in 1926–1940; (c) declining growth rate again in 1941–1945; and (d) explosive population increase in 1946–1960.

The labor force in the economy as a whole increased at the rate of 1.51 percent per year from 1895 to 1960. This was far less than the increase in total population. The percentage of the labor force in the total population, accordingly, declined from 50 percent in 1895 to 32 percent in the period 1956–1960. The agricultural sector had 78 percent of the total labor force in 1895; a figure which declined to 58 percent by 1956–1960. The agricultural labor force increased at an average rate of 0.90 percent and the nonagricultural labor force at 2.77 percent per year during the whole period. The growth rate of the agricultural labor force was 0.59 percent in the period 1911–1915, increasing to 1.61 percent in the period 1931–1935, and then declining to −0.18 percent in the period 1956–1960. The growth rate of the labor force in the nonagricultural sector accelerated from 2.45 percent in the period 1911–1915, to 3.73 percent in 1936–1940, and to 3.68 percent in 1956–1960. The impact of population growth on food production was moderate in the earlier period 1895–1930 but quite substantial in the later period 1950–1960.

The increase in per capita food production throughout the period allowed an increase in both wage rate and the living standard of labor. With higher living standards, nutrition and medical care improved, and the death rate declined.

Taiwan was able to surmount the problems of rapidly increasing population pressure by increasing labor productivity through substantial technological change throughout the period. Table 5 presents data relevant to this process.

In the three periods depicted in Table 5 the rate of population growth accelerated from 1 percent per year to 3 per-

Table 5. Population growth and economic turning point, Taiwan, 1911–1960 (in percent)

Period	Total population growth rate (r)	Techno-logical change rate* (g)	Production elasticity Labor (α)	Capital (β)	Land (γ)	Growth rate of output and capital $G(Y) = G(K)$	Growth rate of labor productivity $G(Y/N) = G(W)$	Growth rate of cultivated land area $G(L)$
1911-15—1926-30	1.00	1.02	0.27	0.12	0.62	1.45	0.45	1.16
1926-30—1936-40†	2.50	1.94	0.25	0.20	0.55	3.21	0.71	0.83
1950-55—1956-60	3.00	2.58	0.28	0.26	0.46	4.62	1.62	0

* In this case, neutral technological change, constant returns to scale, and the law of diminishing returns of production factors are assumed. Solow's model for measurement of technological change was used for computation:

$$\dot{A}/A = \dot{Q}/Q - W_L \cdot \dot{N}/N - W_N \cdot \dot{L}/L - W_K \dot{K}/K$$

where A is technology, Q is production, L is land, N is labor, and K is capital. To smooth the fluctuation of quantity in inputs and outputs, five-year averages of data were used for the estimate. The estimate was limited to the first approximation. The statistical data for computation are quoted from Hsieh and Lee, "An Analytical Review of Agricultural Development in Taiwan —An Input-Output and Productivity Approach," *Economic Digest Series No. 12* (Taipei, Taiwan: Joint Commission on Rural Reconstruction, July 1958).

† For years 1941–1949 see asterisked note, Table 1.

cent per year while the rate of growth of the cultivated land area dropped from over one percent to zero.

The analysis in Appendix B specifies the precise conditions of agricultural development and rising labor productivity in situations of high population growth and land scarcity. Three factors were of prime importance for Taiwan's success in meeting these conditions: the rate of technological change (g) as noted in Appendix B increased nearly as rapidly as population; the production elasticity of land decreased in an unproportional manner when compared with other factors, indicating land saving technological progress; and capital intensification and consequent improvements in the productivity of labor became more important than the quantity of labor in increasing output. This point becomes clear when the production elasticities of labor and capital set forth in Table 5 for the period 1911–1915—1926–1930 and for the period 1926–1930—1936–1940 are compared. In both periods production elasticity of labor declined slightly, but production elasticity of capital increased rapidly. From equations (13) and (14) in Appendix B, it is clear that large increases in production elasticity of capital generally result in high growth of output and labor productivity. Table 5 indicates that the growth rate of output has been faster than that of population in all the three periods and that labor productivity has increased through time. Taiwan's economy, fortunately, has never fallen into the Malthusian trap, and agriculture has accomplished its important role in economic development.

Historical Growth Path of Agricultural Productivity and Technological Progress

One of the striking features of agricultural development in Taiwan is the changing importance of various factors of production and technique in different periods. As the nature of the development and resource availabilities changed, the nature of the development process changed. Some of these features are illustrated in Figure 3.

Productivity of agricultural labor expressed in 1935–1937 T$ is represented by the contour lines, while the coordinates represent the two factors affecting labor productivity: land productivity, and land area per worker. Land productivity

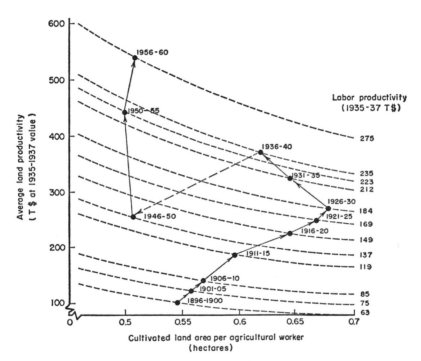

Figure 3. Historical growth path of labor productivity in Taiwan's agriculture, 1895–1960. For the years 1941–1949 see asterisked note, Table 1.

Source: The statistical data for computation are from S. C. Hsieh and T. H. Lee, "An Analytical Review of Agricultural Development in Taiwan," *Economic Digest Series No. 12* (Taipei, Taiwan: Joint Commission on Rural Reconstruction, 1958).

is in turn a function of (a) the amount of capital used per unit area of land and (b) the productivity of capital. The total period divides itself into four segments, each with sharply different characteristics. There are three periods of rising labor productivity and one of declining labor productivity.

As indicated in Table 5, the first period shows cultivated land increasing at a higher rate than the growth of agricultural labor. Capital efficiency decreases rapidly due to the increasing capital investment per unit of land area. Land productivity increases, but at a low rate. We can define this as traditional agriculture. In the second period there is great population pressure on the cultivated land; however, capital efficiency maintains a slow rate of decline despite the increase in capital intensity. As a result, land productivity increases to a higher level at a moderate rate of growth. This period exemplifies the general case of agricultural development. The third period is a special one in which regression of development is seen occurring under high population pressure and disinvestment in agriculture.

In the fourth period, population pressure on land is great but stationary, indicating the same rates of increase or decrease in agricultural labor and cultivated land. Increase in labor productivity depends on rapid increase in land productivity, as was also the case in Japan's agricultural development.

From the above we can generalize two important concepts about the pattern of agricultural development: (a) that the historical growth path of per capita agricultural production has variations; this is contrary to the current economic growth theory which describes monotonic increases in both output and input through time; and (b) that under different conditions of population growth and land resource endowment, different patterns of development are feasible; however, increasing average land productivity is of primary concern for raising per capita income in agriculture. The average labor productivity and average land productivity show a high correlation.[1]

TREND IN THE QUANTITY AND EFFICIENCY OF AGRICULTURAL INPUTS

The close relationship between per capita labor income and average land productivity is more fully seen by observing changes through time in the magnitudes and efficiency of production inputs. Such changes in agricultural inputs in Taiwan in the past sixty years are shown in Figure 4.

Land. Among the factor inputs, cultivated land area increased at the slowest rate. The rate of growth declined over time, reaching a maximum total acreage in 1958, and then it declined in absolute amount.

The expansion of crop area, however, was quite significant in the period from 1945–1960. Often two or three crops can be grown in a year on the same land in Taiwan. Therefore, so long as capital resources permit, crop area can be increased more easily than cultivated land area. Furthermore, crop area as a whole is also affected by changes in acreage planted to perennial and short-term crops. For instance, the growing period of sugarcane is usually about fifteen to eighteen months. In the same amount of time it is possible to grow two crops of rice plus one other crop. The shifting of acreage from sugarcane to short-term crops, which is mostly influenced by the long-range changes in demand and in the pattern of domestic food consumption, results in an increase in the total crop area.

[1] The regression equation of labor productivity with respect to land productivity has been computed as $Y = 36.14 + 0.46X$, $S\sigma = 0.0167$, $R^2 = 0.88025$, where Y is the average labor productivity and X the average land productivity.

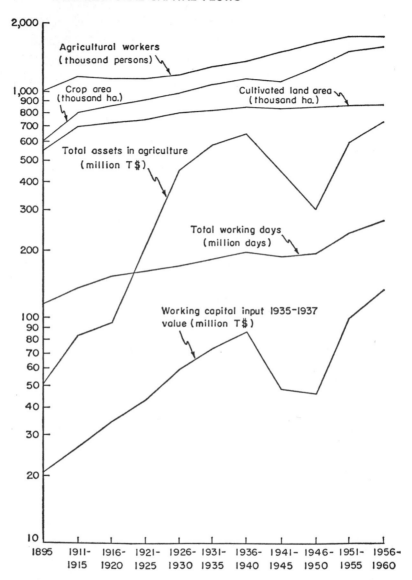

Figure 4. Changes in agricultural inputs in Taiwan, 1895–1960.
Source: Statistics for agricultural inputs have been compiled for a previous study, S. C. Hsieh and T. H. Lee, "An Analytical Review of Agricultural Development in Taiwan," *Economic Digest Series No. 12* (Taipei, Taiwan: Joint Commission on Rural Reconstruction, 1958).

Irrigation. Irrigation is essential in Taiwan because the culture of rice dominates the economy, and the annual rainfall is uneven in distribution. The steep topography and short and rapid rivers also make flood control indispensable. The total acreage of irrigated land increased from 172 thousand hectares in 1895–1900 to 566 thousand in 1956–1960. In the postwar period, total irrigated land area has not increased, despite large investment in irrigation in this period. This is due largely to the shift to more intensive use of irrigated land and the consequent need for more water per hectare of land. The relative changes in the areas of cultivated land, paddy land, and dry land thus reflect the effect of investment in irrigation.

Rada and Lee have reported high correlation $(r = 0.84)$ between the increase in irrigated land acreage and the increase in multiple cropping index with cross-section analysis in 1960. The regression equation indicates that a one percent increase in the irrigated acreage would result in a 1.164 percent increase in the cropping index. Investment in irrigation has been an essential element of increased land productivity and expansion of the cropped area.[2]

However, the importance of technological change to realization of the full benefits from irrigation are clear from Figure 5 which illustrates the radical change in the relationship between increase in the percentage of cultivated area irrigated and land productivity from the period 1911–1925 to the periods of 1926–1940 and 1950–1960. The effect of increased irrigation is much greater in the later periods which have the benefit of technological change.

Labor. The agricultural labor force in Taiwan increased

[2] E. L. Rada and T. H. Lee, "Irrigation Investment in Taiwan," *Economic Digest No. 14* (Taipei, Taiwan: Joint Commission on Rural Reconstruction, 1963), pp. 23–24, Table 14.

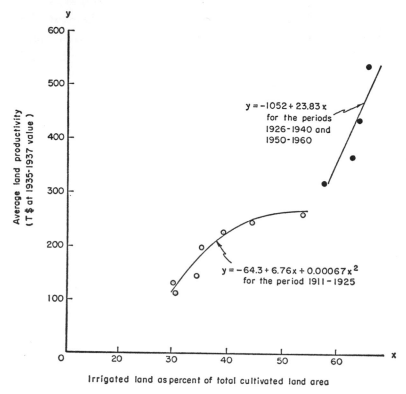

Figure 5. Relationship between average land productivity and irrigation rate in the first, second, and third phases of Taiwan's agricultural development, 1895–1960.

by about 72 percent during the sixty-five-year period from 1895 to 1960. However, as was noted earlier, the average annual growth rate of the agricultural labor force was about 0.90 percent, far below the annual growth rate of the nonagricultural labor force at 2.77 percent. Particularly in the postwar period, the total number of agricultural workers was comparatively stable and maintained a level of around 1.7 million. This was possible because of an increase in the rate of labor outflow from the agricultural sector.

The relationship between the rate of labor outflow from the agricultural sector and the cash wage ratio between agriculture and industry have a close positive correlation ($r = 0.7756$) through the entire period. A high rate of labor outflow was associated with a relatively high cash wage in agriculture, and vice versa. The causal relationship between the two factors has been discussed in detail by Woytinsky, Parsons, and Umemura.[3] The evidence suggests that when job opportunities are available in the nonagricultural sector, the supply of labor from the agricultural to the nonagricultural sector will increase because of the surplus of labor in agriculture. In the dynamic process of economic change when there is inflation or heavy investment in industries, agricultural cash wages generally go up faster than industrial cash wages. The cash wages in agriculture were relatively high in the periods 1911–1915, 1936–1940, and 1956–1960, when there was economic prosperity and rapid inflation. Thus, relatively low per capita income in agriculture provides a potential for labor outflow to the nonagricultural sector. However, the actual labor outflow from agriculture is determined by job availability or investment activities in the nonagricultural sector.

Viewing the relationship between the land and the labor input, it is noted that farm operations in Taiwan were characterized from the beginning by an intensive use of labor. This is to be attributed to the unfavorable land-man ratio. According to the study of Hsieh and Lee, average labor input per hectare of land, which was only 195 man-days in 1911–

[3] W. S. Woytinsky et al., Employment and Wages in the United States (New York: Twentieth Century Fund, 1953), p. 488; also H. L. Parsons, Impact of Fluctuation in National Income on Agricultural Wages and Employment (Cambridge: Harvard University Press, 1952), p. 34; also Matazi Umemura, Chingin, koyō, nōgyō (in Japanese) [Wage, Employment and Agriculture] (Tokyo: Taimeido, 1961), pp. 196–198.

1915 and then increased to 305 man-days in 1956–1960, shows an increasing trend through the whole period.[4] The annual average working days per farm worker increased from 117 man-days in the period 1911–1915, to 143 man-days in 1926–1930; decreased to 115 days in 1946–1950; and then increased again to 155 man-days in 1956–1960. Total days of labor input in agriculture increased quite rapidly from 135 million man-days in 1911–1915 to about 268 million man-days in 1956–1960, an increase of 98 percent.

Capital. Input of capital into the Taiwanese agriculture can be separated into two items: working capital and fixed capital. Working capital includes fertilizer, feed, chemicals, and miscellaneous items. Among these, chemical fertilizers are the most important. Input of such working capital increased over five times from 1911–1915 to 1956–1960 (Figure 6).

Chemical fertilizers were first distributed to sugarcane farmers free of charge by sugar companies because they could not convince the farmers to buy them. In 1903, two years after the introduction of chemical fertilizers, the sugar companies stopped the free distribution but still subsidized farmers in their purchases of chemical fertilizers. In 1904 all imports of fertilizers were coordinated by the Taiwan Governor General's Office. In 1916 fertilizer subsidies to sugarcane farmers were discontinued. The idea and practice of chemical fertilization were soon diffused to farmers who grew other crops. The efforts of the Governor General's Office to improve fertilization practices in rice fields were less vigorous. Use of organic matter and green manure was encouraged in coordination with extension of improved cultivation tech-

[4] Hsieh and Lee, "An Analytical Review of Agricultural Development in Taiwan—An Input-Output and Productivity Approach," *op. cit.*, Appendix Table.

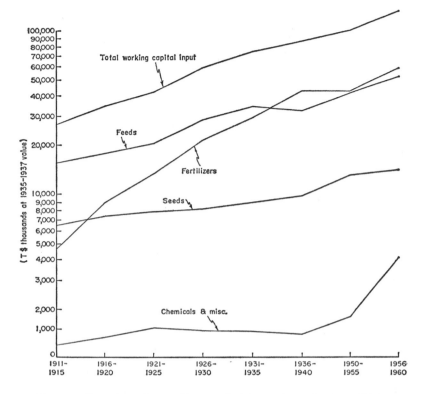

Figure 6. Trend in the working capital input in agriculture, Taiwan, 1911–1960. For the years 1941–1949 see asterisked note, Table 1.

Source: S. C. Hsieh and T. H. Lee, "An Analytical Review of Agricultural Development in Taiwan," *Economic Digest Series No. 12* (Taipei, Taiwan: Joint Commission on Rural Reconstruction, 1958).

niques of rice farming. During this period native rice varieties underwent selection, and the Japonica type was introduced. After 1926, cultivation of rice was rapidly extended in Taiwan, and heavy chemical fertilization of rice fields began. This rapid increase in the use of fertilizers required changes in crop variety and improvement in cultivation practices. It was discovered, for example, that the new variety of Ponlai rice was more responsive to chemical fertilizers than were the native varieties.[5]

Three important economic facts can be identified from the statistical data regarding heavy fertilization of Ponlai rice: (a) the price of Ponlai per M/T was T$17.13 higher than that of the native variety; (b) intensive cultivation of Ponlai rice with heavy fertilization and labor input was more profitable by T$21.58 per hectare when compared to the native variety; (c) if return to family labor is included, the profitability of Ponlai rice production increased by T$40.31 per hectare. The shift in technique from extensive farming to intensive farming was economically profitable in the sense of higher labor return.[6] Fertilizer consumption increased when the utilization of the Ponlai variety became diffused in 1920. The correlation between per hectare yield and consumption of chemical fertilizer on Ponlai rice is +0.92814.[7]

The total quantity of chemical fertilizers applied to rice, sugarcane, and other crops thus reached its prewar peak in 1938, while the average yield per unit of crop area also broke its record. After the postwar restoration, to supply chemical fertilizers was considered one of the most important responsibilities of the government. Encouragement of domestic production of chemical fertilizer together with imports raised the average consumption of chemical fertilizers per hectare from 554 kg. in 1936–1940 to 758 kg. in 1956–1960.

In summary, innovation in Taiwan agriculture is characterized primarily by increased use of fertilizer combined with extended use of new crop varieties. The economic profit-

[5] Kawano, *Rice Economy of Taiwan*, p. 76, Table 27.

[6] Taiwan Governor General's Office, *Taiwan beikoku seisan-hi chōsa* (in Japanese) [Survey Report on Rice Production Cost] (Taipei, Taiwan, 1928), pp. 11, 13, 17, 19, 50, 64, 156, 188, 249, 257.

[7] Kawano, *Rice Economy of Taiwan*, p. 86.

ability of innovation persuaded farmers to move from extensive cultivation in the early period to intensive cultivation with heavy fertilization and labor input in the period 1926–1940. There is another reason for such success with heavy fertilization of crops on Taiwan. Fertilizer requires a relatively small capital outlay and permits application in variable quantities by small farmers. As farmers in Taiwan are predominantly small operators usually handicapped by small acreage and shortage of capital, this innovation is of special significance to agricultural development in conditions similar to those of Taiwan.

As shown in Table 6, total fixed capital in Taiwan's agriculture increased first and then decreased in the period from 1926–1930 to 1936–1940, and again increased rapidly from 1936–1940 to 1956–1960. Among the components, farm buildings increased most rapidly, and irrigation facilities ranked second. Irrigation and land reclamation played a particularly important role in the period from 1911–1915 to 1926–1930. In later periods investment in animals and orchards increased rapidly.

The components of investment expenditure can be classified into three categories—labor, agricultural products, and industrial capital goods—and indicate the varying pressure on different parts of the economy. As seen in Table 7, there is no clear trend in the composition of investment fund expenditure although there are some changes in composition depending on the form investment takes. The increase in investment in animals and orchards in the late period falls heavily on agricultural products. The expenditures on irrigation and land reclamation in the early period fall mostly on labor and industrial goods. Investment in large farm implements, which grew in importance in the later periods, is uniquely dependent on expenditure on industrial goods.

Table 6. Types of fixed capital investment in agriculture, Taiwan, 1911–1960
(in T$thousands for 1911–1940 and NT$thousands for 1950–1960 at current value)

Period	Irrigation	Farm building	Farm tools	Cattle and trees	Land reclamation	Total fixed capital
1911–1915	737	864	29	976	602	3,207
	23%	27%	1%	30%	19%	100%
1916–1920	1,669	3,864	198	8,104	1,785	15,619
	11%	25%	1%	52%	11%	100%
1921–1925	6,735	9,064	2,736	8,894	1,679	29,108
	23%	31%	9%	31%	6%	100%
1926–1930	11,181	10,382	4,541	6,075	1,377	33,556
	33%	31%	14%	18%	4%	100%
1931–1935	3,092	11,943	1,604	6,647	726	24,012
	13%	50%	7%	28%	3%	100%
1936–1940*	2,142	14,636	3,038	23,476	1,288	44,581
	5%	33%	7%	53%	3%	100%
1950–1955	45,106	149,081	62,302	525,178	6,882	788,548
	6%	19%	8%	67%	1%	100%
1956–1960	503,657	1,676,804	343,486	946,400	1,595	3,471,942
	15%	48%	10%	27%	.04%	100%

Source: Based on the unpublished data, "Total Agricultural Assets," estimated by Rural Economics Division, Joint Commission on Rural Reconstruction, Taipei, Taiwan.
* For years 1941–1949 see asterisked note, Table 1.

Data on sources of investment financing indicate a declining trend in the role of government and landlords in agricultural investment (Table 7). Farmers bear proportionally more responsibility for agricultural investment in the later period. In the relationship between investment by farmers on the one hand, and by government and landlords

Table 7. Expenditures and sources of gross agricultural investment, Taiwan, 1911–1960 (in percent)

Period	Total agricultural investment	Expenditure			Sources		
		Labor	Agricultural products	Industrial capital goods	Farmers	Landlords and others	Government
1911–1915	100	49	30	21	72	10	18
1916–1920	100	32	52	16	73	20	7
1921–1925	100	41	31	28	80	10	10
1926–1930	100	48	18	34	71	19	10
1931–1935	100	38	28	34	84	13	3
1936–1940*	100	26	53	21	86	12	2
1950–1955	100	20	66	14	96	1	3
1956–1960	100	38	27	34	97	1	2

Source: Appendix A.
* For years 1941–1949 see asterisked note, Table 1.

on the other, the former have to some degree been persuaded to invest by the government subsidy and the land-tenure system. In most cases of irrigation investment, 50 percent of the total cost was given to the farmers as subsidy. A low-interest loan was also provided in the prewar period. The subsidy was reduced to 30 percent in the postwar period. To encourage the use of improved hog sties, warehouses, and better farm implements or tools, a subsidy system was common in the early period. Ishikawa has defined this relationship between investment response of farmers and government investment by the term investment inducement coefficient.[8] Taiwan's agricultural development policy has been characterized by a high investment inducement coefficient for government investment in agriculture.

Although judicious investment of capital has been made in the agricultural sector, and rapid growth has been achieved in agriculture, it is only in the period 1921–1930 that as much as 14 percent of the total investment went to agriculture (Table 8). In other periods agricultural investment

Table 8. Allocation of capital to the agricultural sector, Taiwan, 1911–1960 (in T$millions at 1935–1937 value)

Period	(1) Total investment in the economy	(2) Agricultural investment	(3) Col. (2) as % of Col. (1)
1911–1915	29	1	3
1916–1920	31	2	5
1921–1925	35	5	14
1926–1930	52	8	15
1931–1935	76	5	6
1936–1940*	89	5	5
1950–1955	151	4	2
1956–1960	242	18	7

Source: The estimate of national capital formation was made by the commodity flow method. For the application of this method to the Japanese case, see Miyohei Shinohara, "Capital Formation in Japan," Keizai kenkyū, Vol. 4, No. 1 (Tokyo, Japan, January 1953), pp. 27–36; also, Henry Rosovsky, Capital Formation in Japan, 1868–1940 (New York, 1960), pp. 156–269.
* For years 1941–1949 see asterisked note, Table 1.

averaged between 2 percent and 8 percent of the total.

This survey of Taiwanese agricultural growth and its modus operandi can be summarized rather simplistically as

[8] Shigeru Ishikawa, "Kaihatsu katei ni okeru nōka rōdō jikyu" (in Japanese) [Farmers' Labor Supply in the Development Process], Keizai kenkyū (Tokyo, January 1965), p. 40.

follows. There was a continuous outflow of labor from the agricultural to the nonagricultural sector which brought about a decline in the relative share of the agricultural sector. Increases in agricultural production resulted more from increases in productivity than from increases in the size of land and labor inputs. However, contrary to the current growth models, neither the productivity of these inputs nor the per capita production showed a monotonically increasing trend. There was considerable variation in the rate as well as in the direction of their movements. The increase in the productivity of land and labor was due to technological changes and increases in the intensity and efficiency of inputs. For one instance, irrigation facilitated multiple cropping, and, for another, increased production as well as increased profitability per unit of input resulted from the use of chemicals and fertilizers, feed, seed, tools and equipment, and increased labor input per hectare.

If we say that the basic development measures necessary for increasing agricultural production and consequently increasing the net real capital outflow from the agricultural sector are capital accumulation and technological progress in agriculture, then when we consider using the Taiwan pattern of agricultural development in other less well-developed countries, we must first recognize and consider that each developing country will inherit somewhat different types of capital accumulation and technology depending on its history, resources, level of technological development, government policy, and population growth. Therefore, although there is a general development pattern for all countries, an effort must be made, when applying the principles set forth here, to identify the components of the specific development pattern for each country.

CHAPTER 5

Transfer of Net Real Surplus
from the Agricultural Sector

In the previous chapter the processes and patterns of growth in agricultural production were analyzed to show their relationship to ways of increasing the net real capital outflow from the agricultural sector. The increase and the means of increase in agricultural productivity determine the potential for net real capital outflow from agriculture. The actual extent to which that potential is realized depends upon measures adopted for mobilization and transfer of capital. It should be recalled from the discussion in Chapter 2 that the visible net real capital outflow from the agricultural sector is determined by the net outflow of food and raw materials to the nonagricultural and the foreign trade sectors. The invisible net real capital outflow is determined by the terms of trade between agriculture and the rest of the economy. In this chapter we will deal with the visible and invisible net real outflows of capital from agriculture.

Determinants of the Sale Ratio

Sale ratio is closely related to the visible net real capital outflow from agriculture. At the micro level the sale ratio is equal to one minus the farmer's consumption ratio of agricultural production. At an aggregate level, sale ratio of total agricultural products is the percentage of agricultural production sold domestically and abroad, and paid as land rent and taxes. Sale ratio thus also has a relationship with the Engel's coefficient, i.e., with the income elasticity of demand for agricultural products by farmers.

Figure 7 indicates the relationship between the sale ratio of total agricultural products and total agricultural production in Taiwan through the three periods. It is clear from the figures that the relationship between the sale ratio and total production varied in the three periods. Roughly speaking, the increase in the sale ratio in Period 1, 1911–1930, was closely related to the increase in the total production. In Period 2, 1930–1940, the sale ratio remained almost constant despite the increase in the total agricultural production. The small fluctuations in the sale ratio in each year were negatively correlated with the changes in total agricultural production. The sale ratio had no relationship at all with the total agricultural production in Period 3, 1950–1960. These changes in the relation between sale ratio and total agricultural production can best be understood by examining changes in the various components that constitute the sale ratio.

The sale ratio of total agricultural products as defined above is allocated to the nonagricultural and foreign trade sectors to supply the current and future food and raw material needs as well as land rent and taxes. Quantities allocated to the food and raw material consumption of the nonagricultural and foreign trade sectors are determined by market forces which directly foster or curtail the quantities sold by cultivators in the market, and indirectly cause a structural change in the agricultural economy thus affecting the quantities consumed and sold by farmers. These two categories affecting cultivators' allocation of production between consumption and sale are by no means mutually exclusive, nor are they independent in the statistical sense of

Total agricultual output (T $ millions at 1935-1937 value)

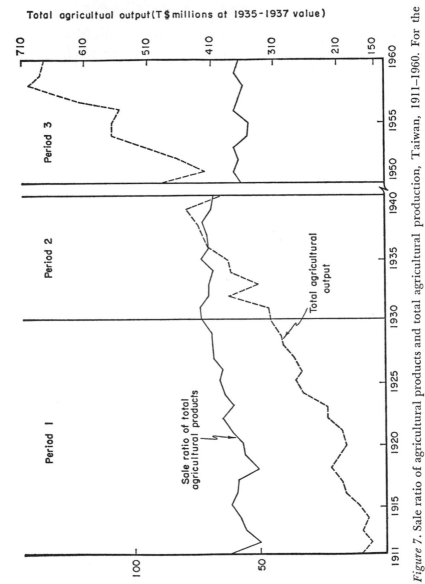

Figure 7. Sale ratio of agricultural products and total agricultural production, Taiwan, 1911–1960. For the years 1941–1949 see asterisked note, Table 1.

Source: See Table 1.

the term. However, one could roughly classify relative prices of various agricultural commodities as being in the first category, and factors such as crop composition, monetization and commercialization of the agricultural sector, tastes and preferences, income distribution, and trends in agricultural production as of the latter type. Sale ratio may also be affected by policies of the domestic and foreign governments and by various other factors that influence quantities exported and through them agricultural production itself. Although quantities allocated to land rent and taxes are determined by institutional arrangements that are beyond the control of the cultivator, they are of interest because in the short run, they affect the surplus extracted from a given agricultural production and, in the long run, stimulate or retard growth of the agricultural sector.

CHANGES IN THE SALE RATIO

Farmers produce rice which is the main food in Taiwan for their own consumption, for payment of rent and taxes, and for sale. Numerous factors determine the quantity of rice disbursed under each of these categories. The relationship between the trends in the sale ratio and in the total production of rice is not identical through the entire period, as seen in Figure 8. Comparing Figure 8 with Figure 7, however, the patterns of change and the trends of both sale ratios are quite similar, indicating that the sale ratio of the total agricultural products is strongly affected by changes in the sale ratio of rice.

In order to analyze the factors influencing changes in the sale ratio of rice, the distribution of rice produce and its quantities sold are estimated primarily from the available statistics. Three important facts about distribution of rice can be noted from Table 9. First, distribution of rice produce

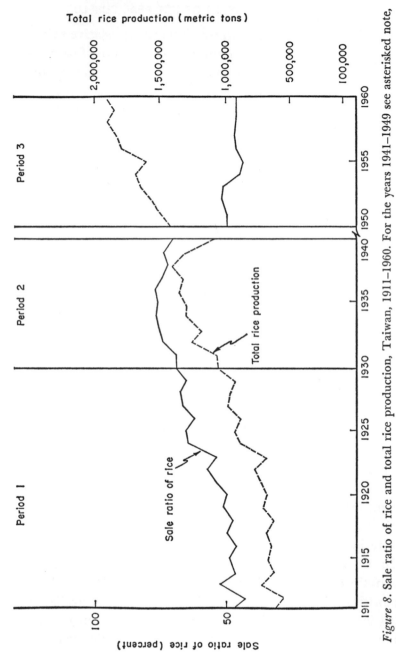

Figure 8. Sale ratio of rice and total rice production, Taiwan, 1911–1960. For the years 1941–1949 see asterisked note, Table 1.

Source: See Table 9.

to landlords was about 27 to 32 percent of the total rice production through the prewar period. Second, as land rent constituted between 27 and 32 percent of the total rice production, any increase in the cultivators' share was dependent on the rapidity with which rice production increased. Third, in the postwar period, government collection of rice has for the most part replaced collection by landlords.

As seen from the last column of Table 9, the sale ratio of rice in 1911–1915 was about 48 percent, increasing to 66 percent in 1926–1930 and further to 74 percent in 1931–1940 and then declining to 46 percent in 1956–1960. In addition to changes in total production during this period, there were changes in farmers' consumption, prices, tenure system, and in the government's collection system, all of which influenced mobilization of rice surplus.

Cultivators' Sales of Rice. One important influence on rice production and its sale has been the farmers' desire for cash. The farm economy shifted from a barter orientation to that of a monetary format when the tax system altered its form of payment from goods to money. The establishment of the monopoly system for tobacco and wine, and the agricultural sector's demand for manufactured goods were other influential reasons for the new emphasis on cash. A need for cash for such expenditures was a primary motivation for commercialization of rice production. The transformation was also brought about by the introduction of chemical fertilizers and capital goods inputs into production, and by increased education and improvements in living standards. The steady increase in rice yield and the lessening of risks helped lead to the increased sale ratio of rice.

In order to clarify the supply response of rice cultivators, simple and partial correlations between the quantity of rice sold by cultivators and total rice production and real rice

Table 9. Distribution of rice in Taiwan, 1911–1960 (unit = 1,000 metric tons of brown rice)

Period	Total production	Distribution		Collection by government (3)	Sale quantity of cultivators (4)	Total sale (5) = (1) + (3) + (4) (5)	Sale ratio of rice (× 100 = %)
		Landlords (1)	Cultivators (2)				
1911–1915	659	182	477		137	319	48
1916–1920	682	225	458		114	339	50
1921–1925	794	267	527		204	471	59
1926–1930	965	324	641		314	638	66
1931–1935	1,229	418	810		500	919	74
1936–1940*	1,304	412	893		561	967	74
1950–1955	1,571	132	977	463	175	784	50
1956–1960	1,858	85	1,257	516	252	854	46

Source: Taiwan Provincial Food Bureau, *T'aiwan liang shih yao lan* (in Chinese) [Taiwan Food Statistics Book] Taiwan, 1960 edition. Estimate of distribution to landlords is based on the following formula: Total land rent paid in rice = average rent paid for the first and second crop × tenant paddy land area for planting first and second crop. Average land rent paid for the first and second rice crops after 1937 is quoted from the annual Provincial Food Bureau, *Taiwan beikoku seisan-hi chōsa* (in Japanese) [Survey Report on Rice Production Cost]; before 1937, average rent for paddy land is quoted from Taiwan Governor General's Office, *Taiwan, jei-mu nen-pō* (in Chinese) [Annual Report of Taxing], annual issue; paddy land area under land-tenure system is quoted from Taiwan Governor General's Office, *Tochi bun-pai to liyo chōsa* (in Japanese) [Survey on Land Distribution and Utilization], five year reports since 1922; paddy land under tenure in the other years was estimated by extrapolating and interpolating. Collection of rice by the government includes land tax, public land rent, compulsory purchase, barter exchange, and repayment for production. Governmental collection and disposal of rice are actually not equal, due to changes in rice stocks from year to year, changes which are not reflected in the table. Governmental collection and disposal figures for rice are from the Provincial Food Bureau, *Liang shih yeh pau tyan* (in Chinese) [Monthly Food Accounting]. Quantity of rice sold by cultivators was estimated from the total quantity retained by cultivators reduced by quantities utilized for consumption, seed, and feed for poultry and hogs. This estimate is based on annual Joint Commission on Rural Reconstruction reports: "Estimate on Rice Disposal" and "Food Balance Sheet of Taiwan."

* For the years 1941–1949 see asterisked note, Table 1.

price in the two periods 1911–1930 and 1931–1940 were estimated by least-squares analysis.[1] From the time-series analysis, cultivators' behavior in the sale of rice can be summarized as follows: (a) when production increase maintained a constant rate or when production remained at a normal harvest level, cultivators' sale of rice was not greatly related to the price change in Period 1 (see Figure 8). Factors other than real price were more important in cultivators' decisions regarding the sale of rice. As the rice yield, both of the first and second crops, showed great year-to-year fluctuations in Period 1 there were considerable changes in rice stocks which exercised a great deal of influence on the quantities of rice sold in that period;[2] (b) the above relationship changed remarkably in Period 2 (Figure 8). The fluctuations in rice yields lessened significantly.[3] Inventory adjustment of rice did not seem as important in this period. Cultivators' decisions about sale of rice in Period 2, however, seem rather strongly determined by the income effect on their consumption.

As for the cultivators' response to price, they were more sensitive to price in the second period than in the first. The factors influencing the cultivators' sale of rice can thus be separated into two different categories: (a) precautionary motive given the uncertainty of annual rice yield; (b) income effect leading to substitution in consumption of crops other than rice. Economic factors affected production and

[1] See Appendix A for details of statistical analysis.

[2] Kawano, *Rice Economy of Taiwan*, p. 93. Kawano estimates coefficients of fluctuation from the trend line production to be 6.84 percent and 8.67 percent for the first and second crop respectively. The coefficients are for the period 1902–1914. For the period 1914–1924 similar coefficients were 5.97 percent and 7.49 percent.

[3] Kawano, *ibid*. The fluctuation coefficients of rice yield were only 3.99 percent and 3.77 percent for the first and second crop respectively.

on-farm consumption of rice, and consequently the extent of commercialization varied in the two periods. However, when real price of rice is assumed constant, the quantity of rice sold was closely related to the size of production in both periods. This relationship implies that increasing rice production was the most important method of increasing marketed surplus of rice under stable price conditions. The sale ratio was also affected by the size of the farm, number of persons per family, and consumption patterns of farm families.

In studying Taiwan's experience, it is assumed that cultivators' consumption is determined by: (a) the magnitude of the squeeze ratio on agriculture as determined by land-rent and land-tax including the compulsory collection of agricultural products; (b) cultivators' desire to repay debts and to hold assets (especially land) ; and (c) cultivators' desire to improve their low-level living standards.

It is to be noted that the squeeze ratio is variable and plays a dual role in the intersectoral capital flow by: (a) balancing the fund of investment and savings between agriculture and the rest of the economy; and (b) mobilizing agricultural surplus in physical terms. Therefore, in analyzing income distribution within the agricultural sector, the role of the squeeze ratio must be taken into consideration, and the structural change in income distribution in the different periods must be emphasized.

Table 10 indicates the changes in net farm income, distributed to landlords and moneylenders, cultivators, and government. Cultivators include owner-operators, tenants, and others who are landlords and owner-operators and/or tenants simultaneously. In Periods 1 and 2 the ratio of total agricultural income distributed to cultivators was roughly in the range of 65 to 67 percent with a slightly increasing trend. This was largely due to the fact that the increase in land-rent lagged behind increase in agricultural productivity. The ratio of farm income distributed to landlords and money lenders declined from 28 percent in 1916–1920 to 25 percent in 1936–1940. The government's share of farm income through taxing and investment repayment was largely constant in both periods.

Table 10 also shows that the income distribution within

Table 10. Distribution of farm income, Taiwan, 1911–1960 (in T$millions for 1911–1940 and NT$ millions for 1950–1960 at current value)

Period	Total agri-cultural produc-tion	Net farm income	Landlords and money lenders	Cultivators	Government and other public institutions
		Period 1			
1911–1915	98	83	22	55	6
		(100%)	(27%)	(66%)	(7%)
1916–1920	188	153	43	101	9
		(100%)	(28%)	(66%)	(6%)
1921–1925	243	195	52	128	15
		(100%)	(27%)	(66%)	(8%)
1926–1930	297	225	59	150	16
		(100%)	(26%)	(67%)	(7%)
		Period 2			
1931–1935	291	220	56	147	17
		(100%)	(25%)	(67%)	(8%)
1936–1940	509	390	98	262	30
		(100%)	(25%)	(67%)	(8%)
		*Period 4**			
1950–1955	7,215	5,448	532	4,204	712
		(100%)	(10%)	(77%)	(13%)
1956–1960	16,035	11,801	739	9,610	1,453
		(100%)	(6%)	(81%)	(12%)

Source: See Table 1.
*For period 3 (1941–1949) see asterisked note, table 1.

agriculture in Periods 1 and 2 tended to favor cultivators slightly, but more than 32 percent of the net farm income was still shared by noncultivators. The government did not play a significant role in mobilizing agricultural surplus through taxing in either period. Since the land reform in 1953, income distribution within agriculture has changed, and the share of landlords in farm income has declined sharply. The percentage of farm income distributed to landlords and moneylenders was 10 percent in 1950–1955 and only 6 percent in 1956–1960. Share of cultivators in farm income increased to 77 percent in 1950–1955 and 81 percent in 1956–1960. Government and public institutions have increased their share to 12 and 13 percent in Period 4. As will be seen later, the rather slow increase in the cultivators' share in farm income in the prewar period and a relatively rapid increase since the land reform has influenced the increase in the real per capita consumption of cultivators throughout the entire period 1911–1960. Per hectare yield of rice increased generally more rapidly than land rent in terms of rice, and the cultivators' real income increased both in monetary terms and as percentage of farm income. This suggests that cultivators' real income can be raised by increasing agricultural productivity through time, even if agriculture has surplus labor and is under a rigid land-tenure system.

Changes in Per Capita Real Farm Income and Consumption. To obtain comparable levels of per capita real income and consumption of cultivators throughout a long period, the effects of changes in agricultural prices and in population involved agriculture have been eliminated.

Per capita real income of cultivators, on the basis of 1935–1937 average price, increased from T$45 in 1911–1915 to T$85 in 1936–1940 or by about 88 percent in thirty years (Table 11). In the fourth period (1950–1960), it declined

Table 11. Per capita real farm income and consumption of cultivators, Taiwan, 1911–1960 (in T$ at 1935–1937 value)

Period	(1) Per capita real farm income	(2) Per capita real consumption	(3) Per capita real consumption of self-produced food	(4) Col. (2) as % of col. (1)	(5) Col. (3) as % of col. (2)
			Period 1		
1911–1915	45	44	25	97	57
1916–1920	55	49	27	88	56
1921–1925	65	56	27	86	48
1926–1930	68	60	27	89	44
			Period 2		
1931–1935	76	69	27	90	39
1936–1940	85	75	27	88	36
			Period 4*		
1950–1955	77	65	31	85	47
1956–1960	101	72	32	71	44

Source: See Table 1.
* For Period 3 (1941–1949) see asterisked note, Table 1.

to T$77 in 1950–1955, and then increased to T$101 in 1956–1960.[4]

Per capita real consumption increased more slowly, from T$44 in 1911–1915 to T$75 in 1936–1940, or by 71 percent. In the fourth period, it increased by 9 percent as compared with 31 percent in per capita real income in the same period. An accelerated rate of increase in cultivators' savings is indicated by the failure of per capita consumption to increase at a rate equal to the increase in per capita real income (Table

[4] A more rapid increase in agricultural population than in agricultural labor force was the main cause of the decrease in per capita real income in 1950–1955.

11). Thus as long as agricultural production increased at a more rapid rate than population, supply of agricultural surplus increased through time.

In the postwar period, income distribution was sharply changed by the land reform program. In 1936–1937, the numbers of farm families who were owner cultivators, semiowner cultivators, and tenants constituted 31, 31, and 38 percent of the total number of cultivators respectively. After the land-reform program in 1954, these figures changed to 57, 24, and 19 percent. In addition to the change in farmers' categories, rent per hectare of land also declined to 37.5 percent of the total product. The redistribution of income through the land-reform program and land-rent reduction raised the average level of food consumption to the high level previously reached by owner and semiowner cultivators. Although the land-price repayment was imposed on new owner cultivators, the payment was far below the increase in the income of the tenants. The rapid increase in per capita real consumption of self-produced foods in this period reflected income redistribution and the upward increase in real income. Such rapid increase in per capita real consumption of self-produced food, together with a high growth rate of population in the agricultural sector, caused the sale ratio of agricultural products to decrease to a large extent in this period.

SALE RATIO, DISTRIBUTION OF RICE PRODUCE, AND LAND-TENURE
SYSTEM OF RICE FARMING

In the period prior to World War II, landlords of Taiwan not only were the sole receivers of rent, but also were important agricultural investors. Their investments in irrigation and land improvement, and their efforts to extend new technology, were aimed at attaining a higher return to land. The land-tenure system, therefore, exercised a great influence on the sale ratio through its role in increasing agricultural productivity and in the distribution of agricultural income and products in Taiwan.[5]

During this period land value, land rent, yield per hectare, and price of the produce were all interrelated and showed an interesting relationship with Taiwan's development. In prewar years, the per hectare value of paddy land increased at 2 percent per year while the per hectare annual yield grew at the rate of 1.4 percent per year. Per hectare land rent increased at an even lower rate of 1.2 percent per year. During the same period the ratio of total land rent in kind to the total rice production increased from about 27 percent in 1911–1915 to 32 percent in 1936–1940.[6] The major increase in the total land rent was due to expansion in the tenant farm area, because per hectare rent increased only slightly. The land share in agricultural income on tenant farm land (defined as land-rent yield) maintained a remarkably stable but noticeably high ratio of around 83 to 86 percent from 1915–1940.[7] The increase in land value in the long run, however, was not significantly associated with improvements in the terms of trade of rice.[8] These economic indicators have important implications. In order to maintain such a large share of land in the agricultural income it was essential for

[5] T. H. Lee and H. T. Chen, "T'aiwan nung-yeh so teh fen-p'ei kou tsao" (in Chinese) [Distribution of Agricultural Income in Taiwan], in Ho-tsua chieh (in Chinese) [Cooperatives, No. 26] (Taipei, Taiwan: Cooperative Bank of Taiwan, 1958), pp. 3–4.

[6] Appendix A.

[7] This was due to mutually opposite trends in two economic parameters. Rate of land rent defined as a ratio of land rent and yield showed a declining trend while the land coefficient, defined as ratio of the value of land and yield, showed an increasing trend. (See Appendix A for further elaboration of concepts and their measurement.)

[8] T. H. Lee and H. T. Chen, "Distribution of Agricultural Income in Taiwan," op. cit., pp. 3–4.

landlords to undertake investment and technological improvement in agriculture in the early period, since any increase in land rent was largely dependent on the increase in land productivity. The system then siphoned off a large amount of surplus from the agricultural sector through the mechanism of rent. In this sense, the tenure system in Taiwan has made a great contribution to the generation and mobilization of agricultural surplus.

The landlord's portion of the marketed surplus of rice was estimated at about 51 percent in the period 1911–1915, increased to 60 percent during 1916–1920, and then declined to 36 percent in 1936–1940. Although the relative share belonging to the landlords showed a declining trend, their total supply increased by the same amount as the land rent in kind (see Table 9).

GOVERNMENT AND THE SALE RATIO

Compulsory collection and rationing of rice was undertaken by the Japanese government in 1942 as a result of the shortage of food in the Japanese Empire during World War II. In the immediate postwar period, this policy of control was abandoned by the Chinese government, even though the large influx of population from the Chinese mainland caused continued food shortages. However, the need for supplies of rice to the government and for additional government revenues brought a series of measures for government acquisition of rice. Land tax and compulsory purchases continued. In 1948 the Provincial Food Bureau established a system of exchange of chemical fertilizers for rice. Land reform (completed in 1953) was combined with a plan designed to secure rice on government account. The amount of rice collected through various government programs is shown in Table 12.

From 1950 to 1960 the government collected more than

50 percent of the rice sold and more than 30 percent of the total rice produced. This percentage surpasses the landlords' share in the prewar period and was enough to control the rice market (see Table 9).

In the period 1950–1960, with the exception of 1955 and 1959, rice production increased by about 50,000 M/T per year. Sale ratio of rice in this period showed a declining trend when compared with the increasing trend in the prewar period. It declined from 51 percent in 1952 and 1953, to 46 percent in 1960. After the land-reform program, the percentage of rice sold by landlords in the total sale of rice was only 10 percent and declining. Government interference in the rice market also declined from 1955. Conversely, the cultivator's share in the sale of rice increased steadily from 13 percent in 1955 to 37 percent in 1960.

Table 12. Government collection of rice, Taiwan, 1950–1960
(unit = 1,000 metric tons of brown rice)

Period	Land tax and compulsory purchase	Barter exchange	Other collection through loan	Land price repayment	Total
1950	155	228	4		388
1951	157	194	43		393
1952	144	260	25		429
1953	141	279	50	26	496
1954	140	287	115	12	554
1955	128	310	34	65	519
1956	132	323	37	28	520
1957	143	349	21	22	535
1958	145	339	19	41	505
1959	113	326	23	51	543
1960	134	293	23	16	466

Source: Taiwan Provincial Food Bureau, *Taiwan ryanshi tongchi yaoran* [Taiwan Food Statistics Book], 1950–1960, and *Ryanshi yeh pau pyan* [Monthly Rice Accounting], 1950–1960.

Since the government's role in the rice market was so important during this period, it would be worthwhile to examine the government collection program for rice. In the immediate postwar period (1946–1950), the purpose of governmental policy was to achieve self-sufficiency in rice production to meet increasing requirements; in the second postwar period (1950–1960), to resume export of rice following further increase of rice production in Taiwan.

Collection of Rice through Land Taxes and the Paddy-rice-barter-exchange System. In collecting rice the government adopted a variety of measures. Some of the devices employed included collection of rural land taxes and surtaxes in kind, and compulsory purchase was made by the Provincial Food Bureau at an official price which was only two-thirds of the wholesale market price for rice.[9]

In addition, barter programs were set up mainly in connection with chemical fertilizers and were designed to collect the bulk of government rice directly from cultivators.[10] As we have seen in Chapter 4, the rate of fertilizer application was particularly high in rice production. Both per hectare and total consumption of fertilizers increased substantially

[9] It is said that the official purchasing price was jointly decided by the Provincial Government and the Provincial People's Assembly in consideration of general commodity prices and the cost of living indices of government officials at the time. However, Jensen reported that actual and planned compulsory sale collection for the whole period under review were never in harmony (B. M. Jensen, *Rice in the Economy of Taiwan,* The Report for FAO Mutual Security Mission to China [Taipei, Taiwan, August 1953], pp. 16–17).

[10] Rice-fertilizer barter exchange could be either spot or loan, but repayment for loan was in kind. The barter program was started with the second rice crop in 1948 and was undertaken on an area basis by the district offices of the Provincial Food Bureau; actual distribution and collection was handled by the township farmers' associations which acted as agents for the Food Bureau.

in the postwar period, and increases in rice yields showed a close relationship with the increase in fertilizer application.[11] The barter program of fertilizer distribution, by offering high exchange rates of fertilizer for paddy, encouraged the demand for fertilizers, and increased yields, and hence resulted in further marketable surplus.

The demand for fertilizers was highly responsive to price changes.[12] The exchange rates between different fertilizers and paddy were pegged by the Provincial Food Bureau and were adjusted from time to time. The exchange rates of fertilizer for paddy, which were quite high, were determined by a monopolistic decision to maximize profits, not by domestic production costs nor by import prices and handling charges.

Made possible by the farmers' demand for fertilizers, the barter system, however, is an economically inefficient method of squeezing surplus from agriculture, but factors presumably political in origin prevented use of other measures to collect more rice from farmers. The commodity barter programs, generally, have been a failure. They have not attained even 50 percent of their goals due to a decline in market prices and unrealistic rates of exchange. Considering the failure of barter programs for cotton cloth and other ne-

[11] Chien-shen Shih *et al.*, "T'aiwan fei-liao huan-ku ti yen-chiu" (in Chinese) [An Appraisal of the Fertilizer-Rice Barter System in Taiwan] (Taipei, Taiwan: College of Law, National Taiwan University, 1961), pp. 20–25. Regression equation relating yield of rice to fertilizer use during 1947–1959 explained 84 percent of the variability in yield due to fertilizer use. A. B. Lewis explained in similar analysis for the period 1952–1964 that as much as 98 percent variability in yield was due to fertilizer use (A. B. Lewis, "The Rice-Fertilizer Barter Price and the Production of Rice in Taiwan, Republic of China," *Journal of Agricultural Economics*, No. 5 [Taichung, Taiwan, June 1967], pp. 127–179).

[12] See Appendix A for statistical evidence relating the elasticity of fertilizer demand and price changes.

cessities, it is clear that the fertilizer barter program was successful largely because of the government's monopoly on fertilizer and the farmers' strong desire to obtain it.[13]

Another program launched for collection of rice was the production loan program which also failed in its early period. Despite the failures in the commodity barter system and loan program, the Provincial Food Bureau has retained these programs in slightly altered form in order to maintain some amount of rice collection. The total collection of rice through the loan program, however, has rarely exceeded 30,000 metric tons.

Collection through Payment of Land Price. The Land-to-the-Tiller Act stipulated that payment of land price should be made in paddy for paddy fields and in cash for dry land.[14] The total amount of land purchased through this program

[13] M. T. Chu, Chairman of the Provincial Farmers' Association, has assessed the profit of the Provincial Food Bureau from the operation of the fertilizer barter program (M. T. Chu, "Fei-liao huan-ku chih-tu ti chien-t'ao" (in Chinese) [An Assessment on Fertilizer Barter System], in *Nung-you* (in Chinese) [The Farmer], No. 3, Taiwan, 1962, pp. 10–12). The total profit of the fertilizer barter program roughly amounted to NT$423 million (equivalent to US$10 ½ million) each year, in which NT$388 million were obtained from imported fertilizer and NT$35 million from domestic production. The profit per metric ton of fertilizer did not change very much after 1953; and in 1961 it ranged from NT$789 and NT$1,270. Also see Appendix A for further details on profits from the fertilizer barter program.

[14] The purchase price of land from landowners for resale to tenant farmers is set at 250 percent of the total main crop yield. The tenants who have received the allocated land are required to pay the purchase price within a period of ten years, in twenty installments, including an interest of 4 percent per annum beginning July 1953. Payment of purchase price to the landowner consists of 70 percent in land bonds in kind and 30 percent in public enterprise stockshares. The Land Bank and Provincial Food Bureau were entrusted with the handling of the issuance of land bonds and with collection and payment of land price in kind.

was estimated to be about 162,000 hectares. Through handling of land price, the Provincial Food Bureau would have held 30 percent of land price or about 30,000 M/T of brown rice on hand for each year. However, as seen in Table 12, the actual collection of rice from this program fluctuated from year to year. This was mainly due to delays in payment by new cultivators or in drawings by the landowners. Fluctuations in stocks made the actual amount of rice gained by the government unstable. To prevent irregular management of rice collection and payment, the payment period was confined to six months from a definite date. This program lasted until 1964 as a supplement to the government's collection program of rice. Since the total government collection of rice exceeded 50 percent of the total rice supply in the market, the government was able to manipulate the market at will.[15] The government's stocks, however, did not reduce year-to-year fluctuations in rice prices.

SALE RATIO OF OTHER MARKETABLE CROPS

Although rice has historically been the main crop in Taiwan, agricultural production has been diversified to some extent in recent years. In the years from 1895 to 1900 sugarcane ranked second to rice in production. Between 1931 and 1940 fruits, fiber crops, and livestock became important. In the postwar period, crops grown earlier continued to increase in importance while many special export crops developed rapidly. Except for sweet potatoes and vegetables, most of the new products were cash crops for which the sale ratios ranged from 70 to 100 percent.[16]

[15] The government's release of stocks was usually confined to the first half of the calendar year. The end-of-the-year stocks with the government, therefore, had considerable influence on the price of rice in the following January–May period.

[16] See Appendix A for details on price policies adopted for cash crops.

CROP COMPOSITION, EXPORTS, AND SALE RATIO

Changes in the sale ratio in Taiwan were strongly influenced by crop composition and its relationship to the exports. Changes in the relative share of crops and livestock in total agricultural products are shown in Table 13.

From 1911–1915 to 1916–1920 miscellaneous food crops including sugarcane, tea, peanuts, and fruits showed an increase in their relative importance, while major grain crops decreased and other crops remained stable. From the beginning of the century until the beginning of World War II, Taiwan's exports which consisted mainly of sugar, rice, and fruits, also increased substantially.[17]

The heavy exports of rice from Taiwan, which were made chiefly to Japan, were due to Taiwan's comparative advantage in rice production. Production cost of rice in Taiwan was only about 57 percent of that in Japan in 1939.[18]

This situation altered significantly after World War II when domestic requirements for food and raw materials became the most important incentive for increasing agricultural production. Production of exportable sugar decreased rapidly, while that of rice, special crops, vegetables, beans, and livestock products increased substantially. Both commodity and geographical concentration of exports declined in the postwar period. Agricultural and processed products as a percentage of total exports declined from 87 percent in 1939 to 68 percent in 1960. The decline in the relative share of agricultural products to total exports can be noted in the movement of the sale ratio in the postwar period (see Figure

[17] See Appendix D for greater detail on the export situation.

[18] A comparison of the production cost or living expenditure of farm labor shows that per capita per year living expenditure was 135.68 in Japan and 99.56 in Taiwan in 1939.

Table 13. Relative importance of crops and livestock in total agricultural output, Taiwan, 1911–1960 (in percent)

| | | | Food commodities | | | | | | |
| | | | Staple foods | | Auxiliary foods | | | | |
Year	Total output	Total food	Rice and wheat	Other grains	Vegetables	Fruits	Miscellaneous food	Meat, livestock, and poultry products	Special crops
1911–1915	100	99	61	7	1	1	15	13	1
1916–1920	100	99	55	7	2	2	20	13	1
1921–1925	100	99	55	7	4	3	18	12	1
1926–1930	100	99	54	7	4	3	19	12	1
1931–1935	100	99	56	7	4	4	17	12	1
1936–1940	100	99	52	7	4	4	21	11	1
1941–1945	100	99	53	8	4	3	23	9	1
1946–1950	100	99	58	10	6	3	13	8	1
1951–1955	100	97	55	8	5	2	14	12	2
1956–1960	100	98	52	8	6	2	15	14	2

Source: Rural Economics Division, Joint Commission on Rural Reconstruction. For the classification of crops and livestock and the computation of the index, see S. C. Hsieh and T. H. Lee, "An Analytical Review of Agricultural Development in Taiwan— An Input-Output and Productivity Approach," *Economic Digest Series No. 12* (Taipei, Taiwan: Joint Commission on Rural Reconstruction, July 1958), pp. 20–21.

7). Details concerning commodity and area composition, volume, and terms of trade of Taiwan's international trade and their role in the overall capital formation in the economy are discussed in Appendix D.

SALE RATIO: A RECAPITULATION

In the survey of the factors affecting changes in the sale ratio of agricultural products we have emphasized the role of landlords, cultivators, and government and the way these groups influence price, land-rent payment, consumption, and exports. The analysis was separated into three phases of agricultural development: 1911–1930, 1931–1940, and 1950–1960. In the process of mobilizing agricultural surplus in Taiwan, the function of price mechanism was somewhat distorted by government intervention and a rigid land-tenure system. In the periods 1911–1930 and 1950–1960 cultivators' production and supply response to the change of price were almost negligible. Throughout the period, expansion of production was the most important factor in influencing the cultivators' sale ratio.

Although per capita real consumption among cultivators was not constant, it increased slowly throughout the entire period, and a major part of the increase was allocated to nonfood items. Increased purchases of consumers' goods and farm inputs provided an incentive to increase marketings. At the same time, a change of income distribution in agriculture and the effects of land-rent reduction in the fifties brought about structural changes in cultivators' consumption and pushed up their level of food consumption, and as a result of such rapid improvement in the cultivators' dietary habits, the sale ratio of agricultural products as a whole was greatly reduced.

Throughout the entire period, the increase in rural population was an important factor in reducing agricultural surplus. However, increase in agricultural surplus was not achieved by reducing agricultural population. Increasing agricultural productivity and the institutional squeeze were important in the transfer of agricultural surplus in Taiwan's experience.

In the prewar period, rent constituted a very high proportion of production on tenant farm land and maintained this high ratio throughout the period. The high rent provided an incentive to the landlords to invest in production-increasing expenditures and simultaneously facilitated siphoning off the increments in production. While increased monetization helped mobilization of surplus through market forces in the prewar period, a variety of barter programs devised by the government played a major role in extracting surplus from agriculture in the postwar period. The programs, by stipulating payment of taxes, input prices, and land values in kind, brought more than half of the marketed surplus of rice within the governmental jurisdiction.

Exports of agricultural products constituted a great force in Taiwan's agricultural development. In the prewar period, sugar and rice which held a high comparative advantage under a special trade system with Japan played a leading role in mobilizing agricultural surplus. In the postwar period, trade patterns changed, and diversification of agricultural exports helped to stabilize export earnings. Improvements in the terms of trade and in production techniques of export products were indispensable for expansion of agricultural exports in this period. State control of agricultural exports still played an important role.

*Changes in the Intersectoral Terms of Trade
and Capital Transfer*

In an examination of the relationship between the intersectoral terms of trade and capital flows, the factors that influenced changes in the terms of trade between the agricultural sector and the nonagricultural sector during the process of Taiwan's development can be specified.

With 1935–1937 as the base, indices of prices received and paid by farmers have shown somewhat different rates of growth between 1911–1915 and 1956–1960 as can be seen from Table 14. The whole period can be divided into three

Table 14. Changes in the terms of trade between agriculture and nonagriculture, Taiwan, 1911–1960 (1935–1937 = 100)

Period	(1) Index of prices received by farmers	(2) Index of prices paid by farmers	(3) Terms of trade Col. (2) as % of Col. (1)
1911–1915	60	73	121
1916–1920	92	119	130
1921–1925	102	114	112
1926–1930	103	103	100
1931–1935	80	86	107
1936–1940*	120	123	102
1950–1955	1,405	1,766	126
1956–1960	2,484	2,995	120

Source: See Table 1.
* For years 1941–1949 see asterisked note, Table 1.

phases: 1911–1930, 1931–1940, and 1950–1960. In the first phase, index of prices received by farmers grew at a higher rate than the index of prices paid by farmers. In the initial period 1911–1915, the intersectoral terms of trade were highly unfavorable to agriculture, but improved gradually through time. In the period 1926–1930, the intersectoral terms of trade favored agriculture. In the second phase, the index of prices received by farmers declined rapidly from 103 in 1926–1930 to 80 in 1931–1935 and went up again to 120 in 1936–1940. The index of prices paid by farmers showed only a moderate increase when compared with the changes in the index of prices received by farmers, and resulted in terms of trade only slightly unfavorable to agriculture. In the third phase, the index of prices paid by farmers increased at a higher rate than did the index of prices received by farmers. Consequently, the intersectoral terms of trade were highly unfavorable to agriculture. The terms of trade moved slightly in favor of agriculture in the last five-year period (Table 14).

Judging from the analysis of agricultural development and sale and exports of agricultural products, several factors account for such changes in the intersectoral terms of trade in the different phases. In the period 1911–1920, the intersectoral terms of trade were less favorable to farmers, because this was a period of slow increase in technological innovation and a period of higher prices of production inputs which were caused by the inflationary trend of industrial goods during and after World War I. Rapid increase in the export of rice to the Japanese market after 1920 influenced the average price of agricultural products, since the price of rice was more favorable than prices of current production inputs. In the second phase 1931–1940, export of rice to the Japanese market was restricted by rice export regulations, and prices of agricultural products in general were less favorable than prices of production inputs. In the third phase, government collection and distribution measures intervened in the rice market. The price of rice and then prices of agricultural products went down slightly, but rapid industrialization on the island in this period led to a more rapid decline of relative prices of agricultural inputs. The intersectoral terms of trade became favorable to agriculture through time.

Terms of trade and intersectoral capital flows were related through commodity transactions between the agricultural sector and the nonagricultural sector. The extent to which intersectoral capital flows were influenced by changes in the intersectoral terms of trade was dependent on the amount of commodity trading between the two sectors. The changes in the intersectoral terms of trade per se would not be indicative of the amount of invisible real capital flows. Invisible outflow of capital as shown in Table 15 indicates the amount

Table 15. Terms of trade and capital flows between agriculture and nonagriculture, Taiwan, 1911–1960 (in T$millions at 1935–1937 value)

| | | Net real capital outflow (in T$millions) | | |
| | | | Visible | Invisible |
Period	Terms of trade	Total	outflow	outflow
1911–1915	121	50	41	9
1916–1920	130	62	46	16
1921–1925	112	60	49	11
1926–1930	100	59	59	(−)0.4*
1931–1935	107	89	78	12
1936–1940†	102	89	85	5
1950–1955	126	113	65	48
1956–1960	120	96	38	58

Source: see Table 2.
* Actual figure is −T$407,000.
† For years 1941–1949 see asterisked note, Table 1.

of capital outflow influenced by changes in the intersectoral terms of trade. The total amount of invisible outflow of net real capital showed positive amounts except during the period 1926–1930, indicating that the intersectoral terms of trade were closely related to the direction of invisible capital flow, but not to the amount of invisible capital flow. From the relationship between the intersectoral terms of trade and invisible capital outflows in the periods 1950–1955 and 1956–1960, it is clear that intersectoral terms of trade in 1950–1955 were more unfavorable to agriculture than in 1956–1960, but the amount of invisible capital outflow in 1950–1955 was smaller than in 1956–1960. The amount of nonagricultural goods purchased by farmers in 1956–1960 was larger than that purchased in 1950–1955, and it was responsible for the inverse relationship between the intersectoral terms of trade and invisible capital outflow in the two periods. In the period 1916–1920, the intersectoral terms of trade were extremely unfavorable to agriculture, but the total amount of invisible capital outflow in this period was only 26 percent of the total net real capital outflow. This indicates that the impact of the changes in the intersectoral terms of trade on the intersectoral capital outflows is not likely to be significant in the early period of agricultural development because of the limited amount of nonagricultural goods purchased. Terms of trade were a major factor in determining intersectoral capital flows only in the period 1950–1960.

 CHAPTER 6

Financial Aspects of
Intersectoral Capital Flows

Under the system of exchange economy, intersectoral commodity transactions are generally backed by delivery of money in either cash or credit. Thus the balance of commodity transactions between sectors can be accounted for by changes in the intersectoral terms of trade and by financial measures, which include farmers' deposits and direct investments in nonagriculture, repayment of loans, and payment of land rent to absentee landlords, payment of taxes and fees, and gifts. In reality, such financial adjustment of the net agricultural surplus is highly complex and is determined by the attitudes of the owners of the surplus, their activities in the intersectoral economy, the development of financial organizations, and the taxing system. As the measures of financial adjustment generally change from period to period in one society, and from society to society, it will be useful to consider the mechanism of financial adjustment with respect to the outflow of net agricultural surplus in Taiwan so that the factors influencing the mechanism and process of financial adjustment can be identified.

Mechanism of Intersectoral Financial Adjustment

In the previous chapter the intersectoral capital flow resulting from physical commodity flows and changes in intersectoral terms of trade was studied. The relationship between the commodity flow and the financial flow in relation to the net capital flow between sectors has been indicated as

$$C^n_a + E_a - I_a - C^a_n = B \tag{1}$$

where C^n_a represents agricultural products sold to the non-agricultural sector, E_a the export of agricultural products, I_a and C^a_n the capital and consumer goods produced in the nonagricultural sector and consumed by the agricultural sector, and B is the balance of commodity transactions between sectors or net agricultural surplus. However, the term (B) also indicates financial adjustment related to the net agricultural surplus.

By definition the term (B) can be separated into the following two parts: $R + K$, where R is the balance of current transfer account and K, the balance of capital transfer account. The classification of current and capital transfer is based on the indirect and direct influence of financial adjustment on capital assets incurred by the balance of intersectoral commodities flow. Therefore, the item (R) includes (a) net receipt of wage and salary income by members of farm households from the nonagricultural sector, (b) net income of agricultural subsidiary business or part-time business revenue from the nonagricultural sector, (c) gifts or private transfers from the nonagricultural sector, and (d) current government expenditures on agriculture on the receipt side. The expenditure side of (R) includes (a) net land-rent payment to absentee landlords, (b) interest on loans paid to financial organizations and money lenders, and (c) payment of government taxes and fees.

The item (K) includes (a) loans from financial organizations and money lenders, (b) investment in agriculture by absentee landlords, (c) government subsidy or public investment in agriculture on the receipt side. Expenditures in

(K) include (a) farmers' deposits with financial organizations and with money lenders, (b) repayment of loans, and (c) direct investment by farmers in the nonagricultural sector.

From the above definitions of (R) and (K) the following equation can be developed:

$$C^n_a + E_a - I_a - C^a_n = R + K \qquad (2)$$

Equation (2) indicates two important relationships: (a) the relationship between the net agricultural surplus and the changes which occur in current and capital transfers in the two sectors, and (b) the balance of intersectoral indebtedness.

Table 16 indicates the above-defined relationship in the intersectoral capital flow in Taiwan through time. Because of a lack of statistics for the period 1895–1910, certain items were not recorded, i.e., interest payment, government subsidy to agricultural investment, loans and private investment in agriculture, and farmers' savings. The basic features of Taiwanese intersectoral capital flows can be summarized as follows:

(1) In the initial period, a large percentage of net capital outflow from the agricultural sector originated through current transfer of capital made necessary by financial requirements such as land-rent payments and taxes. Rent paid to the nonagricultural sector accounted for more than 90 percent of the gross outflow of capital through current transfers in the early period. The rental share declined to about 80 percent in the period 1936–1940, and much more rapidly to about 20 percent in the period 1956–1960. Conversely, taxes and levies increased their relative importance in the current gross outflow of capital during the same period.

(2) Capital inflow of wage, salary, and subsidiary business

receipts through current transfers increased through time and accounted for the most important gross inflow of capital from the nonagricultural sector. In the postwar period, this type of capital inflow increased more rapidly.

(3) Capital inflow through capital account increased at a rapid rate in the prewar period. Public investment and subsidy were the most important components up to 1926–1930, and thereafter loans and private investment were relatively important in the remainder of the prewar period. In the postwar period, public investment resumed its important position.

(4) Savings deposits and repayment of loans through capital account increased their importance gradually throughout the whole period. Capital transfer through capital account showed a net inflow of capital through the prewar period, and turned to a net outflow in the postwar period. These facts imply that transfer of capital through capital account has become more important than current transfer in the process of agricultural development. The factors contributing to such changes are (a) increase in farmers' savings deposits and repayment of loans; (b) decrease in rent payments; (c) relatively slow increase in government taxes and fees; (d) rapid increase in nonfarm income; and (e) decrease or slow increase in public investment and government subsidy after the 1920's.

Land-rent payment, taxes and fees, farmers' saving deposits and repayment of loans are the most important means by which financial adjustment of net agricultural surplus is accomplished. The means of taxation and institutional financing are analyzed here, while land-rent payment to the nonagricultural sector has been previously discussed.

Table 16. Financial aspects of intersectoral transfer of capital, Taiwan, 1896–1960 (in T$millions for 1911–1940 and NT$millions for 1950–1960 at current value)

Item	1896–1900	1901–1905	1906–1910	1911–1915	1916–1920	1921–1925	1926–1930	1931–1935	1936–1940*	1950–1955	1956–1960
1. Current account											
(1) Receipts:											
(a) Income from nonagricultural sector	.6	.6	1.4	2.4	7.7	11.8	5.2	9.1	25.5	383.3	1,552.2
(2) Expenditure:	14.9	19.9	23.3	28.4	51.7	66.9	75.2	72.8	128.4	1,243.5	2,191.5
(a) Land rent	13.4	16.9	18.8	21.8	41.9	50.2	57.4	54.9	97.2	409.2	542.0
(b) Interest				.5	.9	1.6	1.8	1.0	1.1	122.8	196.8
(c) Taxes and fees	1.4	3.0	4.5	6.2	8.8	15.1	16.0	17.0	30.1	711.6	1,452.7
(3) Balance = (1) − (2)	−14.2	−19.3	−21.9	−26.0	−43.9	−55.0	−70.0	−63.7	−102.9	−860.2	−639.3
2. Capital account											
(1) Receipts:	.2	1.0	.6	2.0	2.7	6.1	10.1	4.1	7.5	37.8	115.6
(a) Public investment	.2	1.0	.6	.6	1.0	2.8	3.3	.8	.9	21.9	64.8
(b) Subsidy				1.1	.4	.4	.3	.3	1.3	4.3	6.6
(c) Loans and private investment				.3	1.3	2.9	6.5	3.1	5.3	11.6	44.2

(2) Expenditure:			.3	.9	1.0	.8	3.0	6.4		93.7	424.6
(a) Savings deposits and repayment of loans			.3	.9	1.0	.8	3.0	6.4		93.7	424.6
(3) Balance = (1) − (2)	.2	1.0	.6	1.7	1.8	5.1	9.4	1.1	1.1	−55.9	−309.0
3. Capital transfer from agriculture (outflow)	−14.0	−18.3	−21.3	−24.3	−42.1	−49.9	−60.7	−62.6	−101.8	−916.1	−948.3

Source: See Table 1.

* For years 1941–1949 see asterisked note, Table 1.

An Outline of the Taxing System in Taiwan

It can perhaps be said that agricultural development in Taiwan began with the occupation by the Japanese. The social and economic transformation was brought about by the colonial government in the earlier period of occupation. The fact that development was motivated and promoted by governmental direction indicates that public finance played a great role in the development of Taiwan's economy.

Public finance in Taiwan can be classified into four periods according to changes in receipts and expenditures: (1) the first period, 1895–1904, during which Taiwan received subsidy from Japan's central treasury; (2) the second period, 1905–1936, when public financing in Taiwan developed independently; (3) a period of assistance to the Japanese treasury which occurred after 1937 (for the expansion of Japan's military budget); and (4) the Chinese period which occurred after 1950 when public finance was partly assisted by United States economic aid.

As seen in Table 17, public finance in Taiwan expanded very rapidly after 1896. During the forty years from 1896–1937, the total expenditures increased by fifteen times, whereas current receipts increased by more than fifty-four times. This expansion in current receipts reflects the financial success which was achieved by increasing taxes and by other receipts which came as a result of the rapid development in Taiwan's economy.

In the first period, sources of government receipts were not fully exploited. Major reliance was placed on the receipts from land tax and commodity transaction taxes. At the same time expenditures, including current expenses and investments in railways, telephone, telegraph, forestry, monopoly business (wine and tobacco), and land survey, reached a

Table 77. Public finance in Taiwan, 1896–1937
(in T$millions at current value)

| Period | Receipts | | | Expenditure | | | Index of current receipts | Index of total expenditure |
	Current	Spe-cial	Total	Cur-rent	Spe-cial	Total		
1896	3	7	10	6	5	11	100	100
1897	5	6	11	8	3	10	203	198
1901	12	8	20	12	8	19	446	181
1902	12	8	19	11	7	18	253	172
1906	26	5	31	19	6	26	978	237
1907	29	6	35	20	8	28	1,100	260
1912	43	18	60	26	22	47	1,621	441
1914	39	14	53	32	15	48	1,487	446
1916	46	10	56	33	10	43	1,761	398
1919	67	34	100	47	25	72	2,539	676
1921	70	42	112	64	30	95	2,684	884
1924	85	28	114	70	17	87	3,249	811
1926	97	35	132	70	22	92	3,681	852
1928	104	43	148	77	32	109	3,978	1,020
1930	99	31	130	78	32	110	3,754	1,028
1931	93	23	116	77	22	99	3,658	926
1932	97	24	120	74	23	97	3,681	909
1933	101	30	131	79	23	102	3,836	956
1934	111	31	142	87	25	112	4,216	1,085
1935	108	12	120	93	28	121	4,103	1,159
1936	117	16	134	98	35	134	4,470	1,252
1937	142	16	158	111	47	158	5,406	1,463

Source: Taiwan Governor General's Office, Taiwan tokeisho (in Japanese) [Taiwan Statistics], 1896–1937.

tremendous amount. Under the circumstances, subsidy from the Japanese central treasury was considered necessary. Initially a total subsidy budget of T$37,483 thousands was planned for a period of fourteen years, but actually only T$30,485 thousands was granted.

A grant from the central treasury of Japan occupied 72 percent of the total receipts of Taiwan's public finance in

1896 and 53 percent in 1897. The Taiwanese subsidy was 6.6 percent of the total receipts of the central treasury of Japan in 1896 and 4.8 percent of it in 1897. Such heavy subsidy to Taiwan's public finance raised a serious issue in Japan regarding Taiwan's occupation by the Japanese, and the Taiwan government was therefore faced with the need for careful allocation of its limited funds in various investments in an effort to make Taiwan a profitable colony as quickly as possible. A new taxing program, set up in 1902 to bring in revenue sufficient to make it possible to terminate the subsidy from the Japanese central treasury, was largely based on land, income, and commodity taxes, and revenues from monopolies and public enterprises.

Some specific aspects of Taiwan's financial receipts in this period may be summarized as follows: (a) tax receipts were of little importance in relation to total receipts; (b) monopoly revenue constituted a large percentage of total receipts; (c) revenue from public enterprises, such as railways, telegraph, and telephone, increased in relative importance; and (d) a large annual surplus developed.

Land Tax. In the early period of Japanese occupation, land ownership was divided between large and small landlords. Since land mapping and registration were neither correct nor complete, it was not always clear who was legally responsible for the payment of the land taxes. Land survey and reform were instituted, designed primarily with the objective of finding a new legally stable tax source.

After completion of the land survey, land tax revenue doubled in 1904 and tripled in 1905. The percentage of land tax in the total tax revenue was 34.7 percent and 38.9 percent respectively in 1904 and 1905 but represented only 8.7 percent and 11.7 percent of the government's total financial receipts. However, when this percentage is compared with

Japan's land tax which constituted more than 80 percent of the total tax revenue in the period 1888–1897,[1] it is clear that capital transfer through land tax was not as important a factor in Taiwan. Although land tax was the mainstay of total current tax revenue in the early period, its relative importance (excluding special tax revenue) declined rapidly from 38.9 percent in 1905 to 27.6 percent in 1935 and then to 6.5 percent in 1943. Rapid increase in revenue received from the sugar commodity tax beginning in 1904 and from the business income tax after 1937 lessened the importance of land tax as a source of revenue.

Sugar Commodity Tax. To compensate for the decrease and, ultimately, for the suspension of subsidy from the central treasury of Japan, a sugar commodity tax was first imposed by the Taiwan government in 1901. The total amount of sugar commodity tax was only T$370 thousand in 1901, but increased rapidly with the increase of sugar production. By 1910 it amounted to T$12 million and occupied 63.4 percent of the total tax revenue and 21.9 percent of the total government financial revenue.[2] Revenue from the sugar commodity tax made investments in irrigation, flood control, economic survey, development of agriculture in mountainous areas and other social infrastructure possible without issue of government bonds.

Improvement of the Taxing System in 1937. Improvement in the taxing system prior to 1937 can be roughly divided into three periods. In the first period 1895–1913, emphasis

[1] Ohkawa and Rosovsky, "The Role of Agriculture in Modern Japanese Economic Development," *op. cit.*

[2] As more than 80 percent of Taiwan's sugar was consumed by the Japanese, the legal receipt of such consumer tax had become a great issue between Taiwan and Japan. Most Japanese cited this tax as a cause of the modification in subsidy from Japan to Taiwan. A part of the sugar commodity tax had been transferred to Japan after 1911.

was on replacing old tax items inherited from the Chin dynasty with new items, such as customs duty, sugar, textile, and kerosene commodity taxes, business income tax, stamp tax, and issue tax on bank notes. In the second period, 1914–1921, improvement of land tax procedures and establishment of separate systems of local and national tax were the main concerns. Indirect taxes were revised primarily during the third period, 1921–1936. The improvement of the tax system in 1937 had emphasized development of direct taxes. This tax system had two drawbacks in a developmental context: unfair tax burden and inflexibility of taxing. The 1937 tax system improvement had specific purposes: (a) to establish income tax as the main pillar of the tax system; (b) to allocate the tax sources into local and national levels in order to promote local development programs; (c) to establish some new tax items; and (d) to make tax revenue more flexible. Land tax in total tax revenue, including special tax revenue, declined from 23.2 percent in 1936 to only 4.0 percent in 1943, and conversely, income tax including special income tax increased from 25.8 percent in 1936 to 38.7 percent in 1943.

Economic Aid in the Period 1950–1960. The government showed a tremendous budget deficit after the transfer of the national government from mainland China to Taiwan in 1950. Extrabudgetary accounts cover as much as 25 to 30 percent of the total consolidated expenditure of the central and provincial governments. For the most part, these extrabudgetary accounts are related to funds received through use of dollar-aid and corresponding funds in local currency of United States economic aid. According to the estimate made by the United States Agency for International Development, the government debt totaled NT$9.7 billion up to

June 30, 1963, of which NT$5.3 billion was external debt, while the balance was domestic debt.[3]

The national account of the government revenue in current years as seen in Table 18, indicates that the sources of

Table 18. Composition of general government revenue, Taiwan, 1951–1960
(in NT$millions at current value)

Period	Income from property and enterprises	Indirect taxes	Direct taxes*	Current transfer from domestic source	Current transfer from foreign countries	Total
1951	282	1,169	301	170	636	2,558
1952	256	2,000	491	417	953	4,117
1953	192	2,425	623	254	1,311	4,805
1954	165	3,296	617	345	1,442	5,865
1955	325	3,978	814	247	1,410	6,774
1956	685	4,511	915	324	1,013	7,448
1957	804	5,665	841	407	1,449	9,166
1958	884	6,243	948	625	2,032	10,732
1959	1,093	7,062	1,189	631	2,473	12,448
1960	1,339	7,930	1,369	705	3,084	14,427

Source: Directorate-General of Budgets, Accounts and Statistics, Executive Yuan, *National Income of the Republic of China, 1962 issue* (Taipei, Taiwan, 1963), Table X.

* Including income tax, land tax, household tax, deeds tax, house tax, mining lot tax, and estate tax.

domestic revenue were income from property and enterprises and indirect and direct taxes. Tax revenue occupied only about 61 to 65 percent of the total domestic government revenue. Among the revenue sources, customs duties ac-

[3] U.S. Department of State, Agency for International Development, Mission to China, "Economic and Social Trends," unpublished mimeograph (Taipei, Taiwan, 1963), pp. 16–18.

counted for about 20 percent of domestic revenues and monopoly revenue accounted for over 25 percent.

The proportion of direct and indirect taxes shows a ratio of 25:75 on the average, and the relative importance of indirect taxes increased throughout the period. The specific situation reflects a tendency toward decline in the ratio of tax burden to Gross Domestic Product (GDP) from 1955. This implies that the tax system during this period was inelastic when compared with the period 1937–1944.

Functions of Public Finance in Agricultural Development

The role of public finance in agriculture generally has two features: (a) to force capital transfer through taxing, and (b) to direct investment and subsidy to agriculture through its expenditures. Accordingly, the following questions may be asked: (a) What was the tax incidence on farmers as compared with the tax incidence on those in the nonagricultural sector? (b) How did direct government taxes influence the increase in agricultural productivity? (c) How did indirect taxes and nontax devices influence the terms of trade between the agricultural and the nonagricultural sector? (d) What government measures were adopted for increasing agricultural productivity through public expenditures?

COMPARISON OF TAX INCIDENCE BETWEEN AGRICULTURAL AND NONAGRICULTURAL SECTORS

Sectoral tax incidence is related to structural change in an economy first through development in productivity and second through the individual's taxability. For the purpose of analysis, the sectoral tax burden will be discussed only in relation to direct taxes. Direct taxes include land tax, mining tax, income tax, house tax, issue tax on bank notes, and local taxes. Land tax is the most important direct tax on agriculture.

In 1900 the direct tax burden in the agricultural sector accounted for 76 percent of total direct taxes. It increased to 81 percent after the land survey in 1905, declined to 65 percent in 1911, and declined further to 42 percent in 1930. After the tax system reform was undertaken in 1937, the share of direct taxes in the agricultural sector decreased rapidly and accounted for 21 percent in 1940. In the postwar period, the agricultural share of direct taxes increased to 52 percent in 1953, as industrial production recovered slowly from war damage. As a result of industrial development thereafter, the agricultural share of direct taxes decreased gradually to 38 percent in 1960. Generally speaking, agriculture's share in direct taxes shows a declining trend with change in the economic structure consequent upon development.

The following observations may be made concerning per capita direct taxation:

(a) Increase in the per capita direct tax on agriculture was slower than the increase in the per capita GDP in agriculture in the prewar period.

(b) Higher per capita direct tax burden in the nonagricultural sector in the later period (1933–1940) was due largely to the increase in income tax. According to the tax system of the Japanese administration, income tax was imposed only on corporate income, interest revenue from bonds, and other incomes. Since 1896 household tax was imposed on farm households as a local tax.

(c) The low ratios of per capita direct taxes to per capita GDP in the agricultural and the nonagricultural sectors do not mean a low tax burden as a whole, because in the total tax revenue, indirect taxes accounted for 69 to 79 percent of the total.

(d) Since the major direct taxes in the early period were the land and local taxes, the higher direct tax burden in agriculture indicates that taxation had an important role in capital transfer from the agricultural sector. In view of the declining trend in the ratio of per capita direct tax to per caipta GDP in agriculture, it can be stated that taxation did not deter agricultural development. On the contrary, GDP in agriculture increased at quite a high rate. This is, of course, also related to government expenditures on development measures in agriculture. However, two points should be

Table 19. Comparison of tax incidence between agriculture and industry by different income levels, Taiwan, 1933 (in T$ at current value)

Income levels	Taxes paid by farmers	Taxes paid by nonfarmers	Average
400 (or below)	49	47	48
800	113	87	100
1,200	157	158	157
2,000	333	234	283
3,000	522	412	467
5,000	923	624	773
7,000	1,417	833	1,125
10,000	2,018	1,661	1,840

Source: Taiwan Governor General's Office, Bureau of Finance, *Taiwan jei-mu hōkoku* (in Japanese) [Survey Report of Taxes], Taipei, Taiwan, 1933, which has been translated into Chinese in *Taiwan Economic Series No. 8*, Bank of Taiwan, p. 161.

clarified regarding the decline in the ratio of per capita direct tax to per capita GDP in agriculture. The total amount of direct tax in agriculture increased continuously through time. Land tax increased quite rapidly before 1930, and local taxes increased rapidly in the succeeding period.

Despite the decline in the ratio of per capita direct tax to per capita GDP in agriculture in the prewar period, per capita tax incidence was heavier in the case of land tax in the early period and heavier in the case of local taxes in the later period.

(e) With respect to the tax incidence between the agricultural and the nonagricultural sectors and relative individual taxability in the two sectors, the Taiwan government reported that agriculture's share of taxes was heavier than that of the industrial sector, as indicated in Table 19.

Table 19 also indicates that within similar income levels, the tax burden on agriculture was heavier than in nonagriculture. Agriculture thus contributed capital to nonagriculture through taxation.

IMPACT OF INDIRECT TAXES ON AGRICULTURAL PRODUCTION

Indirect taxes under the Japanese administration, such as the sugar-manufacturing tax, sugar commodity tax, tea tax, export tax, monopoly revenue tax, had an important role only in the period prior to 1937.

Because of the dominance of Taiwanese tea and sugar in the international market, taxes on these two items were arranged so that the burden of payment was assumed by foreign consumers. This was also true of monopoly revenue obtained from camphor and opium.[4] Opium, for example, was consumed domestically only by the wealthy segment of the population. Farmers thus suffered little from indirect taxes in the early period. This situation however, changed in the later period under the Japanese administration when the incidence of indirect taxes on cultivators increased.

As export tax revenue was limited in amount and the tax-

---

[4] See Appendix A for distribution of monopoly revenue by items.

ing period was so short, its relative importance in tax revenue was negligible. Tariff revenue, once shifted to the Japanese central treasury in 1911, returned to Taiwan again in 1914. The total amount of tariff revenue reached T$5,161 thousands in 1925—due to a large trade of raw sugar, wheat, and rice. Since then it has declined year by year.

In the postwar period, indirect tax revenue occupied 60 to 65 percent of the total government tax revenue, and its relative importance was similar to that of the early period of Japanese administration. It included commodity taxes, tariff revenue, business tax, stamp tax, amusement tax, slaughtering tax, harbor fee, and monopoly revenue.

Commodity taxes are refunded to producers when goods are exported, and therefore the total revenue is shared by domestic consumers. Business tax, stamp tax, amusement tax, harbor fee, and monopoly revenue for the most part can be said to "shift forward" and are shared by consumers. Due to "shifts" and consequent changes in the domestic terms of trade, the timber commodity tax and slaughtering tax are complex in their impact on domestic production of timber and hogs. A brief analysis of their respective influences will demonstrate their importance.

Timber Commodity Tax. More than 90 percent of the total timber sold was supplied by government enterprises in Taiwan. After World War II, the demand for timber was large as a result of reconstruction to repair war damage. Under the conditions of this excess demand for timber, a 20 percent timber tax could easily be shared by consumers.[5] However, after 1957, a decline in the total sale of timber resulted in excess supply. The timber tax became a deterrent

[5] C. Y. Yien, "Lin-yeh fa-chan ch'u-i" (in Chinese) [Development Measures for Forestry Industry], in *Industry of Free China,* Vol. 14, No. 1 (Taipei, Taiwan, 1955), p. 204.

to an expansion of timber production and to a reforestation plan. The decline of timber production also influenced the government business revenue. After a long debate on this issue, the timber commodity tax was cancelled by the government with a promise of a subsidy from the corresponding fund in the treasury.

Slaughtering Tax. The slaughtering tax on livestock was begun under the Japanese administration with the intention of using tax revenues to increase the agricultural improvement fund in local government. The relative importance of the slaughtering tax in the total tax revenue of local government in this period was not significant, but it became the most important source of tax revenue of local government in the postwar period. The slaughtering tax comprised 14 percent of the tax revenue and 9 percent of total financial revenue of local government bodies in 1950, rising to 35 percent and 17 percent respectively in 1954, and continuing at roughly that level to 1960.

The consumers' price elasticity of demand for pork was −1.4 according to a study of the time-series data through the period 1921–1952.[6] However, the supply of hogs on the farm level could be considered inelastic in terms of current price. The supply is generally related to the real price of hogs 26 months earlier. Such a lag between real price for hogs and the supply from the farm thus constitutes an inelastic demand curve for hogs on the farm. Therefore, if the market margin between the consumers and the grower is widened by the increase in slaughtering tax, the proportion of additional slaughtering tax shared by farmers will be larger than that

[6] T. H. Lee, "T'aiwan mao-chu chia-ke ti yen chiu" (in Chinese) [A Study on Hog Price in Taiwan], in *T'ai Yin chi k'an* (in Chinese) [Quarterly Journal of Bank of Taiwan], Vol. 8, No. 3 (Taipei, Taiwan, 1956), pp. 187–189.

shared by consumers. Thus, slaughtering tax is shifted backward to farmers. Despite the rapid increase in demand and the price of pork in the recent period, slow increase in hog production may well have been strongly influenced by the increase in slaughtering tax.

GOVERNMENT EXPENDITURE ON AGRICULTURE

Government expenditures under the Japanese administration increased quite rapidly in proportion to the increase in total financial revenue. Since the accounting of public enterprises was not separate from the government budget, the expansion of government expenditures included a large proportion of production expenses from public enterprises. To obtain a clear picture of government expenditures alone, an adjustment, shown in Table 20, was made to eliminate monopoly and enterprise expenses from total government expenditure.

There are several important facts to be derived from this table.

(a) Except in 1895, development and subsidy expenditure ranked first under the Japanese administration. In the early period 1902–1921, it accounted for more than 50 percent and declined slightly after 1928. The main items of developmental expenditure were railways, irrigation, harbors, and roads which included other means of transportation. Industry and agricultural expenditures included extension expenditures on rice, pineapple, and silk, agricultural inspection and grading, fishery investigation, and industrial training. Subsidies were allocated to local development funds, navigation, irrigation associations, and agricultural extension. After 1936 these expenditures were provided for under the integrated program of the Ten-Year Industrial Development Plan. These categories indicate that a large percentage of govern-

Table 20. Government expenditures, excluding monopoly and enterprise expenses in the Japanese period, 1895–1937
(in T$millions at current value)

	Administration		Education		Debt payment		Pension		Development		Subsidies		Others		Total	
	T$	%	T$	%	T$	%	T$	%	T$	%	T$	%	T$	%	T$	%
1895	4.5	58	0.4	5					1.9	25	0.6	8	0.3	4	7.7	100
1902	4.2	33	0.3	3					6.1	48	0.9	7	1.4	11	12.9	100
1907	2.9	18	0.3	2	2.3	15			6.0	38	3.6	23	0.7	5	15.9	100
1912	4.3	13	0.6	2	3.1	10			10.9	34	4.2	13	9.3	29	32.3	100
1916	4.1	17	0.8	3					6.8	28	5.4	22	7.3	30	24.4	100
1921	19.2	32	2.4	4	3.4	6			24.4	41	6.5	11	3.5	6	59.5	100
1926	18.0	36	4.4	7	4.6	9			9.5	19	7.0	14	7.5	15	50.2	100
1928	18.8	30	4.7	8	5.2	8			17.0	27	9.1	14	8.8	13	63.7	100
1932	18.1	31	4.8	8	6.1	10	2.6	5	11.8	20	7.1	12	8.4	14	58.8	100
1935	19.4	28	5.1	7	7.6	11	4.9	7	12.8	18	9.0	13	10.5	15	69.4	100
1937	21.5	24	6.3	7	6.7	8	5.1	6	16.9	19	12.3	14	20.4	23	89.2	100

Source: Taiwan Governor General's Office, *Taiwan tokeisho* (in Japanese) [Taiwan Statistics], 1896–1937.

ment expenditure under the Japanese administration was allocated primarily to investment in infrastructure and agriculture.

(b) Since administration expenditure included local government expenditures, the actual percentage of total expenditure would be around 10 percent.

(c) Debt payment fluctuated from year to year and occupied roughly 10 percent of the total expenditure. More than 60 percent of the debt fund was spent on railway construction, 25 percent on irrigation construction, and 15 percent on harbor construction. Therefore, expenditure on debt payment can be accounted as development expenditure.

(d) Education expenditure was low in the early period and increased rapidly after 1920. As education occupied 20 to 30 percent of the local government expenditure, total expenditure on education was not less than 15 to 20 percent of the provincial government expenditure.

In view of the high share for agriculture and infrastructure in the total local government expenditure, it can be safely said that the Taiwanese government emphasized agricultural development in the early period and then shifted to industrialization after 1930.[7]

In the postwar period, the pattern of government expenditures changed greatly. The consolidated statement of government expenditures in central and local governments after the restoration of Taiwan to China indicates that defense expenditure constituted 58 to 70 percent, general administration ranked second at 9 to 13 percent, and education followed at 7 to 13 percent of the total expenditure. Eco-

[7] Tokujiro Kitayama, "Utaka na Taiwan zaisei" (translated into Chinese) [Wealthy Taiwan Finance], in *T'aiwan ching-chi shi pah chi* (in Chinese) [Series of Taiwan Economic History No. 8], (Taipei, Taiwan: Bank of Taiwan, 1959), p. 162.

nomic reconstruction, communication, and transportation comprised only 2 to 6 percent of the total expenditure.

Even at the provincial level the government expenditure on economic reconstruction and communication was only 15 to 20 percent of the total provincial government expenditure.[8] According to the study of government expenditure for agricultural development undertaken by the Joint Commission on Rural Reconstruction, only 4 percent of the total government expenditures was allocated to agricultural investment and improvement. Including agricultural administration, the total agricultural expenditure in the governmental budget was about 5 percent in 1961.[9] However, it must be noted that the government played an increasingly important role throughout the postwar period.

Table 21 shows the general status of agricultural financing in Taiwan in the fiscal year 1961 (FY1961).[10] Attention is drawn to the role played by agencies other than those of the government. The financial assistance by the Joint Commission on Rural Reconstruction in overall agricultural financing is most noticeable. Its FY1961 allocations of fixed capital to agriculture were about three times as large as the total sum provided for agricultural development by the governments at all levels. It was also about 50 percent larger than the total investment made by all agricultural public enterprises, such as Taiwan Sugar Corporation, Food Bureau, and Forestry Bureau, and was about 25 percent more than the funds provided by all farmers' organizations.

[8] Taiwan Provincial Bureau of Accounts and Statistics, *T'aiwan t'ung-chi yao-lan* (in Chinese) [Taiwan Statistical Abstract] (Taipei, Taiwan, 1950–1960 editions), pp. 182–183.

[9] S. C. Hsieh and T. H. Lee, "Agricultural Development and Its Contributions to Economic Growth in Taiwan," *op. cit.*, p. 68.

[10] FY1961 means the fiscal year of government finance from July 1960 to June 1961.

Table 21. Nature of agricultural financing in Taiwan, FY1961
(in NT$millions at current value)

Fund sources	Fixed capital investment	Agricultural improvement disbursements	Administrative expenditures	Agricultural credit	Total
Joint Commission on Rural Reconstruction	321.8	111.1	17.8	80.0	530.7
Grant	124.4	111.1	17.8		253.3
Loan	197.4			80.0	277.4
Government	109.9	90.2	67.0		267.1
National			0.3		0.3
Provincial	45.5	57.9	39.2		142.6
Prefecture/city	46.3	22.3	12.5		81.2
Township	18.0	10.0	15.0		43.0
Agricultural public enterprises	203.8	41.8		562.0	807.6
Banking				1,408.8	1,408.8
Farmers' organizations	255.0	15.8		645.2	915.9
Private farms	653.8				653.8
Total	1,544.2	258.9	84.8	2,695.9	4,583.8

Source: "Statistical Review of Agricultural Financing in Taiwan and JCRR Contributions," unpublished report of Joint Commission on Rural Reconstruction, Taipei, Taiwan, December 1961.

Of the total expenditure on various agricultural improvement projects, appropriations by the Joint Commission on Rural Reconstruction were NT$111 thousand or about 43 percent of the total expenditure in the year.

The above facts show that the provision of funds by the Joint Commission on Rural Reconstruction for agriculture significantly supplements government financing, which has been at an extremely low level, in carrying out various projects.

In conclusion, some important facts about the role of governmental finance in the agricultural development of Taiwan may be discerned:

(a) In the early period of the Japanese administration, the government taxed agriculture heavily, but also provided a large portion of its revenue to develop agriculture. However, the net capital outflow from agriculture through taxation and governmental expenditure was still positive. In the later period, the relative tax burden shared by agriculture decreased. Government appropriation of funds to agriculture also declined. In consequence, net capital outflow from agriculture through public finance increased in absolute terms.

(b) In the postwar period, the tax on agriculture increased rapidly after the land-reform program became operative. But the government's contribution to agriculture through provision of funds was not significant in the total agricultural development fund which included foreign sources. A large development fund for rapid agricultural development in this period came for the most part from the Joint Commission on Rural Reconstruction. Net capital outflow from agriculture through government transfer was also very substantial in this period.

Farmers' Financial Status and Intersectoral Capital Transfer

Apart from the capital outflow through taxation and through financial requisition of rent by landlords, one of the important financial mechanisms of capital outflow from the agricultural sector is the transfer of net savings which takes the form of direct sectoral adjustment in savings and investment. Although net savings and investment in agriculture are related to the level of production, their amounts differ according to the factor proportions in agricultural production, capital efficiency in agriculture and nonagriculture, consumption level, and debt payment of farmers. With respect to the transfer mechanism of net savings from agriculture in Japan, Ohkawa and Shinohara have developed the theoretical approach of a two-sector Harrod Model with assumptions of balanced growth of labor productivity in agriculture and nonagriculture, and a high capital-output ratio in the agricultural sector.[11] These assumptions do not apply, however, in the case of Taiwan.

In order to understand the farmers' financial structure and its relationship to investment behavior in agricultural production, first, agricultural income and expenditures through time will be analyzed. Second, agricultural net savings and investment in agriculture will be discussed in terms of their financial structure. Finally, an effort will be made to investigate the role of the agricultural financial organizations in the intersectoral capital transfers.

THE BALANCE OF AGRICULTURAL INCOME AND EXPENDITURES

On the basis of the estimated social accounts in agriculture presented in Chapter 2, the changes in agricultural income and expenditures through time are presented in Table 22.

The total agricultural income shown in the table is not all money income. It includes agricultural income, nonagricultural income, and wage income from investment in agriculture. The last item of wage income is the estimated value of the labor input in agricultural investment, and thus cannot be transferred through financial mechanism. A notable fact about the total agricultural income is that the share of

---

[11] Kazushi Ohkawa, *Economic Analysis of Agriculture*, pp. 44–46; and Miyohei Shinohara, "Kōgyō no seichō-litu" (in Japanese) [Growth Rate of Industry], in *Nihon keizai no bunseki* (in Japanese) [The Analysis of Japanese Economy], eds. Tsurn and Ohkawa (Tokyo: Keiso, 1955), Vol. I, pp. 72–74.

Table 22. Balance of agricultural income and expenditures, Taiwan, 1911–1960 (in T$millions for 1911–1940 and NT$ millions for 1950–1960 at current value)

Item	1911– 1915	1916– 1920	1921– 1925	1926– 1930	1931– 1935	1936– 1940*	1950– 1955	1956– 1960
Agricultural income	55.0	101.4	127.8	149.5	147.0	261.7	4,204.4	9,609.8
Nonagricultural income	2.4	7.7	11.8	5.2	9.1	25.5	383.3	1,552.2
Wage income from investment (1)	1.6	5.0	11.9	16.0	9.2	11.6	161.3	1,329.2
Total income (2)	59.0	114.1	151.6	170.8	165.3	298.9	4,749.1	12,491.2
Living expenditure on agricultural products	32.8	58.1	63.1	67.0	58.3	94.6	1,896.2	3,953.0
Living expenditure on non-agricultural products	24.3	43.7	67.7	86.6	90.6	168.8	2,108.0	4,925.6
Total expenditures (3)	57.0	101.8	130.8	153.6	148.9	263.4	4,004.2	8,878.6
Surplus (2) − (3) = (4)	2.0	12.4	20.8	17.2	16.4	35.5	744.9	3,612.6
Net savings (4) − (1)	0.4	7.3	8.9	1.2	7.2	23.9	583.6	2,283.4

Source: See Table 1.
* For years 1941–1949 see asterisked note, table 1.

nonagricultural income increased from 4 percent in 1911–1915 to 13 percent in 1956–1960. The nonagricultural income was the current transfer of funds from the nonagricultural sector to the agricultural sector. It is conceptually similar to the land rent paid by farmers to landlords in the nonagricultural sector. However, these two items represent opposite directions of gross fund flow. From our estimate of the two fund flows, it is clear that nonagricultural income increased through time, but land rent paid to the nonagricultural sector increased first and then declined in the later period. Consequently, net fund flow from the agricultural sector to the nonagricultural sector declined as more labor moved out of agriculture and into other job opportunities made available through economic development.

Of the total expenditures, that on nonagricultural commodities was about 45 percent of the total in 1911–1915 and increased to 56 percent in 1956–1960. The average propensity to consume was 96 percent in 1911–1915, 88 percent in 1936–1940, and 71 percent in 1956–1960. If we deduct the wage income in investment (1) from total agricultural income (2) in Table 22, then the average propensity to consume in relation to money income was about 99 percent in 1911–1915, 92 percent in 1936–1940, and 80 percent in 1956–1960. Accordingly, the average money saving ratio was 1 percent, 8 percent, and 20 percent in the respective periods. The low level of money savings in agriculture in the early period seems to have been a result of low agricultural productivity, high rent payment, and taxing. In the 1930's high agricultural productivity, slow increase in farmers' living expenditures, and in land rent were the factors contributing to the increase in savings. The high savings in the 1950's could be largely attributed to income distribution through the land-reform program in 1953.

SAVINGS AND INVESTMENT

Net money savings in the agricultural sector were appropriated for investments in agriculture and nonagriculture. Their proportions changed from period to period. Except for 1911–1915 and 1926–1930 when the ratios were 30 percent and 36 percent respectively, the proportion of total savings invested in agriculture was generally more than 50 percent. The proportion was particularly high in the postwar period and went beyond 80 percent.

Table 23 shows that outflow of money savings from agriculture was not exceedingly large. When we subtract the amount of loans from financial agencies in the nonagricultural sector, the net outflow of money savings from agriculture becomes meager and turns into a net capital inflow in the early period 1911–1935, and then becomes a net outflow thereafter. In order to clarify the allocation of net agricultural savings to agricultural and nonagricultural investments, it will be necessary to study agricultural savings and investment in relation to the changes in the aggregate assets and liabilities in agriculture.

Land constituted about 80 percent of the total capital assets in the period 1911–1920. It decreased to 65 percent in 1936–1940, to about 50 percent in 1950–1955, and then in 1956–1960 it increased to 65 percent. Change in the value of land assets is influenced by increases in land value per hectare and total land area owned by farmers.[12]

[12] Increase in land value per hectare can be attributed to the increases in irrigation investment and consequently to land productivity. House and farm buildings comprised only 2 percent of the total assets in 1911–1915, but increased rapidly to 15 percent in the postwar period. Orchard trees occupied about 7 percent in the early period, but decreased to about 0.8 percent in 1956–1960. Irrigation facilities comprised about 6 percent of the total assets through time. The relative importance of

Table 23. Annual savings, investment, and transfer of capital from agriculture, Taiwan, 1911–1960
(in T$millions for 1911–1940 and NT$millions for 1950–1960 at current value)

Item	1911–1915	1916–1920	1921–1925	1926–1930	1931–1935	1936–1940*	1950–1955	1956–1960
Surplus	2.0	12.4	20.8	17.2	16.4	35.5	744.9	3,612.6
Net savings	0.4	7.3	8.9	1.2	7.2	23.9	583.6	2,283.4
Investment in agriculture	0.1	6.4	7.9	0.4	4.2	17.5	490.0	1,858.7
Outflow of savings (1)	0.3	0.9	1.0	0.8	3.0	6.4	93.7	924.6
Repayment of loans and interest (2)	0.5	0.9	1.6	1.8	1.0	1.1	122.8	542.0
Increase in loans outstanding from nonagriculture (3)†	0.9	1.1	4.1	3.8	9.7	5.2	62.1	239.1
Net outflow of savings = (1) + (2) − (3)	(−)0.3	0.7	(−)1.5	(−)1.2	(−)5.7	2.2	154.3	727.5

Source: See Table 1.

* For 1941–1949 see asterisked note, Table 1.

† The total loans figure from the nonagricultural sector has been reported by Department of Finance, Taiwan Provincial Government, and reproduced in H. Y. Chen and R. A. Bailey, *Agricultural Credit in Taiwan*, Department of Agricultural Economics, Ohio State University, 1966. That amount is nearly twice as large as the estimate in the above table due to the double accounting in the statistics of the Department of Finance. For instance, loans of Land Bank, Cooperative Bank and government agencies are generally committed by Farmers' Associations for its practical management. The amount of the loan was accounted twice by Farmers' Associations and Land Bank, Cooperative Bank, and government agencies. In the above table, loans to agricultural investment through government agencies in irrigation and other improvements were accounted here also.

Investigation to classify the assets according to the nature of investment makes clear that irrigation facilities are the chief government asset, while investment in fixed assets seems more important to farmers. In the early period, investments in orchard trees and livestock, especially cows, were the most preferred by farmers. In the periods 1926–1930 and 1936–1940, investment in farm implements was an

Table 24. Sources of agricultural liabilities, Taiwan, 1933 and 1950 (in percent)

Item	1933	1950
Land bank (Hypothec Bank)	16.4	2.4
Commercial bank	4.6	0.5
Farmers' associations	13.0	19.0
Food bureau		0.8
Landlord	3.3	0.7
Business	5.5	1.9
Sugar company	6.7	0.8
Private money lender	48.8	73.2
Others	1.7	0.7
Total	100.0	100.0

Source: Taiwan Governor General's Office, *Nōgyō kinyū chōsa hōkoku* (in Japanese) [Survey Report on Agricultural Credit], Taipei, Taiwan, 1933; and Taiwan Provincial Department of Agriculture and Forestry, *Nung-yeh shin yon t'iao cha* (in Chinese) [Report on Agricultural Credit], Taipei, Taiwan, 1950.

important concern. In the later period (1950–1960), investment in house and farm building was preferable.

With respect to the liabilities of agriculture as a whole, private lending was the most important source of agricultural financing. Financial agencies constituted 34 percent of

---

livestock declined and that of farm implements increased in the long run. Cash, stock, and deposits seem less important and change in the range of 0.5 to 1 percent of the total assets.

the total agricultural liability in 1933 but only 22 percent in 1950 (Table 24). Among the financial agencies, the land bank (Hypothec Bank of Japan) covered 16 percent of the total in 1933 and decreased to 2 percent in 1950.

Financing by farmers' associations ranked second in importance at 13 percent in 1933, increasing to 19 percent in 1950. In both periods, the land bank, farmers' associations, and cooperative banks were the main resources for agricultural financing. Family consumption was shown to be more important than production in regard to the uses of loans or causes of liability among farmers.[13] The proportion was roughly 60 and 40 percent.

In the early period, the increasing trend in liability among farmers, together with repayment liability, resulted in decrease in outflow of net savings from agriculture. Rapid increase in agricultural savings influenced the increase in outflow of net savings from agriculture in the later period.

The Role of Agricultural Financial Agencies in the Capital Transfer Mechanism

Two agricultural financing agencies in the prewar period were dominant: Hypothec Bank of Japan (the present land bank) and Credit Cooperatives (the present farmers' associations). In the postwar period, the Cooperative Bank was established in addition to the above agencies to bring about financial adjustment of supply and demand for funds between the Farmers' Associations.

As in the newly developing areas or colonial countries, total demand for investment funds was excessively high in

[13] Taiwan Governor General's Office, *Nōgyō kinyū chōsa hōkoku* (in Japanese) [The Report on Agricultural Credit] (Taipei, Taiwan, 1933), pp. 10–15.

Taiwan in the early period, when the country was financially dependent upon Japan. According to the Taiwan Governor General's Office report on "Transfer of Funds between Taiwan and Japan for 1926–1935," there was a net inflow of funds throughout the period. Table 25 indicates that the

Table 25. Flow of funds between Taiwan and Japan, 1926–1935
(in T$millions at current value) *

Period	Inflow of funds from Japan	Outflow of funds to Japan	Net inflow
1926	67.2	40.7	26.5
1927	91.5	30.8	60.7
1928	105.3	47.8	57.5
1929	61.9	42.9	18.9
1930	89.1	67.3	21.8
1931	121.9	58.2	63.7
1932	52.6	50.4	2.2
1933	57.5	47.0	10.5
1934	38.0	38.7	(−).7
1935	37.1	31.5	5.7
Total	722.1	455.2	267.0

Source: The report of Taiwan Governor General's Office as it was reproduced in Kamekichi Takahashi, Modern Taiwan Economy (Tokyo, 1937), p. 586.

* The flow of funds between Taiwan and Japan does not mean the real net amount of capital flow between the two countries.

net inflow from Japan decreased slowly and that net outflow first appeared in 1934. This indicates that the supply of funds in Taiwan did not meet the domestic requirements for funds for a long period. The total demand and supply of funds in the economy as a whole showed an extraordinary gap in the period before 1930. Takahashi has reported that the financial gap was particularly wide in Taiwan's economy because of slow capital accumulation. The specific pattern of Taiwanese savings in landholding was the main reason for such slow capital accumulation.[14]

From the accounts of the financial agencies, it is clear that savings deposits were generally less than the total loans, but this gap has been narrowed through time. The issue of Taiwan bank notes accounted for 30 percent of the share and the remaining 70 percent was brought about by a transfer of funds from the Hypothec Bank of Japan to the branch office in Taiwan.[15] During 1925–1930, transfer of funds from Japan through the Hypothec Bank declined remarkably. In view of the above-mentioned situation of demand and supply of funds in Taiwan's economy as a whole, it might be said that the Hypothec Bank was serving the function of introducing funds into agriculture.

The total amount of deposits and loans in the Hypothec Bank, of course, does not represent all deposits from and loans to the agricultural sector. However, it is very clear from Table 24 that the loans of the Hypothec Bank constituted the largest percentage of farmers' borrowings from financial agencies and also the main source of investment funds under the public sponsorship. The loan policy of the Hypothec Bank also changed the direction of loans from agriculture to industry around 1935 with the result that the introduction of funds into agriculture has decreased since then.

In the years preceding 1913, farmers' financing was dependent largely on private money lenders, landlords, and businessmen. Then in that year fifteen credit cooperatives were established by landlords, cultivators, and rural business-

[14] Kamekichi Takahashi, *Taiwan keizai gendai don* (in Japanese) [Modern Taiwan Economy] (Tokyo: Ganshodo, 1937), pp. 585–587.
[15] Takahashi, *ibid.*

men throughout the entire island, and the total number increased very rapidly to 206 in 1920, to 333 in 1933, and to 421 units in 1940.

Exemption from income tax and other business taxes on their profits was one reason why the rural credit cooperatives expanded so quickly, and it is apparent, also, that the credit cooperatives displayed some usurious characteristics in their conduct of business. The interest rate charge on loans was approximately 1.05 percent per month, and that paid on deposits was 0.51 percent per month. The great margin between deposit and loan rates was for a long time a basic characteristic of the rural credit cooperatives in the Japanese period.[16] The capital stock of the rural credit cooperative was mostly shared by landlords, businessmen, and big cultivators.

According to the report on sources of loans and deposits in rural credit cooperatives in 1940, 43 percent of the loans were released to businesses and only 28 percent of them were for agricultural production. It is clear from the rapid increases in deposits of rural credit cooperatives in other banks and in their reserve that the rural credit cooperatives served the function of adjusting rural financing in its early period and altered their function to siphoning off capital from agriculture after 1930.

In the postwar period, the Hypothec Bank was reorganized as the Land Bank of Taiwan, and the Cooperative Bank of Taiwan was reorganized for the purpose of adjusting the financial status of the credit departments of the former rural credit cooperatives which were associated with the farmers' associations. The actual business coordination be-

---

[16] Hong-yen Chen, *Taiwan no keizai to nōgyō* (in Japanese) [Economy and Agriculture in Taiwan] (Taipei, Taiwan, 1944).

tween the Land Bank, the Cooperative Bank, and the farmers' associations has been negotiated on the basis of loan term and usages of loans. Under the pressure of rapid inflation after World War II, the government fixed interest rates for bank deposits and loans in order to encourage quick recovery and further development of agricultural and industrial production. Credit expansion and issue of bank notes were the main sources of loanable funds; long-term deposits to banks were negligible. Private financing played a great role in this period until financial reform occurred in 1949. Increase in deposits also was encouraged with the incentive of a high interest rate on long-term deposits. Credit expansion was strictly limited by regulations. Time and savings deposits increased quickly and substantially as inflation slowed down.

There is no statistical information for further comparison of the loans and deposits made to and from the agricultural sector by the Land and Cooperative Banks. If farmers' payments for purchase of land are taken into consideration, about NT$700 million in 1954 and NT$3,500 million in 1960 flowed into the Land Bank, thus constituting a large part of loan sources. Installment payment of the loans for investment in irrigation also constituted a large percentage of farmers' savings. This repayment was also officially deposited in the Land Bank. If all surplus funds of farmers' associations were deposited in the Cooperative and Land Banks, the net outflow of funds from agriculture through these financial institutions would be great each year.

Certain important points emerge from the analysis set forth in this chapter. In the early period of agricultural development, 1895–1930, government taxation of agriculture and capital outflow form agriculture through land-rent payment to nonagriculture played an important role in capital transfer from agriculture. As farmers' net savings were generally low and financial investment in agriculture urgent, capital transfer from agriculture through financial institutions was not significant.

In the second period, 1930–1940, and the postwar period, 1950–1960, capital outflow through financial institutions became more important than taxing and land-rent payment. After the land reform in 1953, taxation and outflow of net savings were the important mechanisms of transferring capital from agriculture.

From the above facts, it can be generalized that in the initial period of agricultural transformation, tax on agriculture seems an appropriate means of siphoning off capital from agriculture. In the early period, farmers showed an inclination for holding more fixed assets than cash and deposits. Outflow of net savings is generally directed to debt payment. Since government-organized investment in agriculture plays so important a role in its transformation, agricultural taxation is a necessary measure for collecting such an investment fund. To transfer capital from agriculture to industrial development simultaneously with agricultural transformation, government expenditures on public investment in agriculture must be considered in the context of investment plans and technological change. J. W. Mellor's proposition, which expresses the importance to development of net transfer of resources from the agricultural to the nonagricultural sector and the importance of agricultural taxes as a transfer device, is supported by this case study.[17]

[17] Mellor, "Toward a Theory of Agricultural Development," *op. cit.*, pp. 26–27.

It is apparent, also, that capital transfer from agriculture in the later period of development depends greatly on outflow of net savings through financial institutions. Establishment of the rural credit institutions and a special interest rate policy for their business operations in the early period is necessary.

CHAPTER 7

Implications of
Taiwan's Experience

*Strategic Measures for Agricultural Development and Capital
Transfer*
With a systematic examination of Taiwan's experience
for the period 1895–1960, we set out to provide a statistical
framework for empirical analysis of intersectoral capital flow
between the agricultural sector and the nonagricultural sector. A statistical scale for measuring the intersectoral capital
flows was developed by the social accounting system based on
the definition of capital, and an effort was made to identify
the determinants of the net capital outflow from the agri-
culural sector. Conclusions may be summarized as follows:

(a) The direction of the intersectoral net capital flow was
identified as an outflow from the agricultural sector in Taiwan throughout the entire period. The amount of net capital outflow showed a slightly increasing trend in terms of real
price up to 1940, but has tended to decline since 1950. Invisible net real capital outflow caused by terms of trade
against agriculture was less important in the prewar period
but increased in relative importance to more than 50 percent
of the total net real capital outflow in the postwar period.
Financially, current transfers of rent payment and taxes occupied the most important role in the financial accommoda-
tion of net agricultural surplus in the prewar period, and

direct capital transfer of farmers' savings became increasingly important in the postwar period.

(b) The size of the intersectoral capital flow is dependent in part on the changes in the terms of trade, but it is also significantly dependent on the physical and financial measures by which development can be achieved. Certain measures and conditions significantly influenced the intersectoral capital outflow in Taiwan: (1) Under the Japanese administration a new system of government taxes and levies was imposed while the inherited system of agricultural squeeze was not abolished. Since institution of land-reform program in the postwar period, taxation and levies by means of both direct and hidden methods have been strengthened. (2) Despite the high-gross squeeze, agricultural productivity of land and labor in the sector was not affected. After the shift from traditional agriculture in the period 1926–1930, the increase in agricultural productivity was accelerated. Neither the initial resource endowment nor the level of agricultural productivity in Taiwan in 1895 was any more favorable than in countries presently developing. However, the successful transformation of traditional agriculture in Taiwan could be accomplished while maintaining a continuous net outflow of capital from the agricultural sector. A heavy investment in irrigation was initiated in the transformation period, yet it did not bring a net inflow of capital from the nonagricultural sector with it. This important aspect of agricultural development particularly with reference to the role of government and technological progress in agriculture is discussed below.

(c) The empirical tests showed that Taiwan's experience departed appreciably from the conventional hypotheses regarding net capital outflow from agriculture. (1) Taiwan has maintained a continuous outflow of net capital from the agricultural sector under the high growth rate of agricultural population and labor force. This fact disproves the broadly held viewpoint that decelerating the rate of population growth is a necessary condition for accelerating the growth of agricultural surplus. (2) The agricultural wage rate or per capita consumption of farmers improved through time, despite the increase of population in agriculture. However, the proportion of total agricultural income going to agricultural labor has tended to decline relatively in contrast to the nonagricultural sector where the proportion of total income to labor increased. In the context of net capital outflow from the agricultural sector, the relative decline of the share of labor income in agriculture is thus a more important concept than that of constant institutional wage rate in agriculture. (3) Heavy investment in irrigation is necessary in order to transform traditional agriculture in the paddy farming areas. Intensive innovation in the use of capital has been witnessed in the period of transformation of traditional agriculture. This departs from the conventional viewpoint of a complementary relation between capital and labor in agricultural innovation. (4) As for the amount of net capital outflow, it is clearly shown by the statistical comparison in the text that the concept of "net agricultural savings" is not appropriate. (5) Financial adjustment of the net agricultural surplus is one of the important factors determining the magnitude of the net capital outflow from the agricultural sector. The problem of intersectoral capital flow can be discussed from the viewpoint of financial adjustment and the commodity transferring process as well as from the viewpoint of increase in agricultural productivity.

(d) Finally, agricultural development is primarily concerned with the feasibility of increasing net agricultural surplus or net capital outflow form the agricultural sector. In less-developed countries like Taiwan, mobilization of internal capital must depend on agricultural development. The development of agriculture and the application of economic squeeze on agriculture are closely related to government strategies for agricultural development.

In relation to the intersectoral capital outflow from agriculture, four important government measures toward agricultural development can be derived: (a) allocation of capital to agriculture, (b) technological progress, (c) agricultural taxation, and (d) organizational improvements. The weight of their comparative importance in the different phases of agricultural development may be summarized.

Initial Period of Agricultural Development, 1895–1930. Despite the initial conditions of low land productivity, low average crop yield, and unfavorable man-land ratio in 1895–1900, net outflow of capital from agriculture was positive. Population increased at the slow rate of 1 percent annually. Per capita food consumption of agricultural products in total farm income was 65 to 70 percent, including self-produced and purchased food. High squeeze ratio of land-rent payment was the most important mechanism in transferring capital out of agriculture, while taxation did not play a very important role. Efforts for agricultural development began around 1898 utilizing material inputs and institutional organization. Institutional reform extended to the land-tenure system, land-registering system, farmers' organizations, administration system, agricultural experimental stations, and agricultural education. Material inputs were allocated to survey, inventory, and investment in basic resources.

The ten-year Indica rice-improvement program, government control of the irrigation system, introduction of a new sugarcane variety, and subsidy on chemical fertilizer were the important activities. Capital investment was moderate in the earlier period, 1900–1920. Taxes increased rapidly through land survey and registration. Rent also increased moderately with the slow increase in crop yield. Increase in land productivity in the earlier period lagged behind the increase in labor productivity. There was little acceleration in agricultural productivity and little heavy investment in this earlier period. Net capital outflow from agriculture continued to be positive. The transformation of traditional agriculture continued until 1920.

From 1918 until after World War II, the need for more rice and sugar in the Japanese market preconditioned government behavior; this resulted very soon in a rapid increase in the production of rice and sugar. Internally, the man-land ratio became worse and a big push in land productivity was necessary. The two conditions which determined large governmental investment in this decade were financial possibility and technological feasibility. The government budget showed a surplus, and the landlord class financially supported the government's heavy investment in irrigation and land improvement. A big investment increase in irrigation and land improvement could be expected to be fruitful due to the new Ponlai rice variety and the adoption of chemical fertilizers by farmers. Transformation of traditional agriculture was completed in this decade. More than 50,000 hectares of the Tao-yien canal irrigation area and 150,000 hectares of the Chia-nan irrigation area were completed in 1925 and 1930. A rapid increase in utilization of chemical fertilizers also began in this period. The ratio of total capital goods allocated to agriculture in the decade 1920–1930 was on the average 14.5 percent, marking an historical record. As a result of heavy investment in irrigation in this decade, the proportion of land irrigated increased to 53 percent, land productivity increased by two times, and the total sale ratio of agricultural products reached 70 percent. In financing such heavy investment, landlords and farmers still played an important role. They allocated a large percentage of their additional income to investment. Favorable terms of trade for agriculture and high technological profitability provided an incentive for their participation in investment.

High government taxation of agriculture, increase in land rent, and farmers' autonomous savings helped to maintain a positive net capital outflow from agriculture. In terms of economic relationships, the following five factors worked simultaneously together to cancel the adverse effect on capital tarnsfer of the high rate of capital allocation in agriculture: (a) the high squeeze ratio which included taxes and land-rent payment in total agricultural production; (b) the slow increase in per capita consumption of farmers; (c) the moderate rate of population increase in agriculture; (d) the rapid growth of agricultural exports; and (e) the high technological change and investment multiplier. The organized financial transfer mechanism was *sine qua non* for the effective working of the above five factors.

Transformation of Agriculture and Industrialization in the Period 1930–1940. In this period, the rate of capital growth was negative in agriculture, and the ratio of capital goods allocated to agriculture also declined rapidly to about 5 to 6 percent. Following the successful transformation of traditional agriculture in the later phase of the first period, growth of agricultural land productivity was still at the high rate of 1.9 percent per annum. Technological change accounted for 1.5 percent a year of this figure. Rapid increase in the application of chemical fertilizers was accompanied by the use of new varieties of seeds. More inputs of working capital and labor resulted from the specific character of technological linkage effect on output in this period. The market price mechanisms and technological profitability acted as persuasive incentives for farmers. Small-scale farming, together with organizational help, made adoption of new technology possible at a rapid rate. Autonomous growth in agriculture was systematically established in such a way that the abundant resources of labor and scarce capital funds combined appropriately to increase output and to contribute to industrial expansion. Agricultural development in this period not only contributed agricultural surplus and productive resources for industry, but also provided momentum for economic transformation and scarce resources for use in the two sectors. Net capital outflow from agriculture reached a historical peak in terms of visible funds. The dominant factors were increases in net savings and taxes. Increase in rent payment slowed down. High sale ratio of agricultural products marked the successful achievement of agricultural transformation. Also the system of taxation and financial institutions worked effectively in mobilizing capital out of agriculture.

The principal factors accounting for capital outflow from agriculture in this period may be summarized as follows: (a) high technological progress with more inputs of working capital and labor; (b) decrease in fixed capital goods allocated to agriculture; (c) relatively slow increase in land-rent payment; (d) the time lag between the increase of farmer's per capita consumption and the increase in income; (e) favorable terms of trade for agriculture; and (f) continuously rapid increase in agricultural exports. These factors working together under an organized institutional framework demonstrate the role of agriculture in Taiwan's economic development.

Further Development of Agriculture in the Period 1950–

1960. The basic conditions for agricultural development looked gloomy in the immediate postwar period. Population increased more than 3.0 percent while prospects for expansion of farm land area were limited. Total agricultural output was set back to the 1910 level, mostly because of fertilizer shortages and war damage to irrigation facilities. Taiwan suddenly changed from a food surplus area to a food shortage area during the six years between 1942 and 1947. When Taiwan was ceded to China, its two most important assets were the technically educated farmers and the large number of agricultural organizations. Adequate prerequisites existed for government action on the choice of development measures. A quick recovery and further development of agriculture depended upon a purposeful, progress-oriented attitude by the government. However, the government did not actively participate in a developmental plan until 1948. First, institutional reforms consisting of a land-reform program and reorganization of farmers' associations were launched. Second, scarce materials imported with United States economic aid were allocated to agriculture and industry under the national development plan. Third, highly developed technology was transmitted to farmers through the Joint Commission on Rural Reconstruction.

The price mechanism was not considered as an incentive for adopting new technology and increasing agricultural output. Government allocation of chemical fertilizers, pesticides, irrigation water, funds and subsidy compensated for the price mechanism. Government collection of rice, sugar, and other important products in addition to the unfavorable terms of trade resulted in a tremendous net capital outflow from agriculture. Forced savings from land-price repayment and autonomous savings of farmers were other factors influencing increase in the capital outflow.

The major factors determining the capital outflow from agriculture in this period can be listed as follows: (a) total output of agriculture increased rapidly at more than 4.0 percent per annum, with technological change contributing as much as 2.4 percent. In addition to increasing the rate of per capita consumption, this growth rate far exceeded the population growth rate; (b) during the rapid industrialization at more than 17 percent per annum in this period, the wage rate in industry was two times higher than that in agriculture. The large food requirements of the industrial sector, combined with export demand, provided a major demand potential for agricultural products; (c) the capital-output ratio in agriculture increased to some extent in this period but was still less than the capital-output ratio in the nonagricultural sector; (d) investment in agriculture in this period was accompanied by a large multiplier effect, although the ratio of capital goods allocated to agriculture was only about 5 percent; (e) taxes, forced savings on agriculture, and farmers' autonomous savings constituted a large squeeze on agriculture. However, invisible capital tarnsfer occupied more than 50 percent of the total net capital transfer from agriculture throughout the period.

After all, the effects of the rapid technological change in agriculture and the high squeeze through direct and indirect taxes on agriculture outweighed the inflow of capital and industrial consumer goods into the agricultural sector. The role of landlords in the capital transfer mechanism ceased in this period.

Implications of Taiwan's Experience

In considering the implications of the above discussion, it is important to generalize the relationship between determinants of the intersectoral capital flow in order to provide a measurement of agricultural development. The resource endowment and the level of agricultural productivity determine the size of agricultural investment that can be undertaken to achieve a given rate of agricultural growth. Basically, land productivity and per capita land area or man-land ratio are the determinants of the level of agricultural productivity in terms of labor. Consequently, given the increase in population, limited land resource and heavy food requirements in a low income country, a big increase is required in irrigation and land improvement. For this reason, Ishikawa and Ruttan have concluded that the agricultural sector may require a net inflow of capital from the nonagricultural sector for the transformation of agriculture in Asia.[1] This obviously does not apply to Taiwan's experience, since a big push in irrigation and land improvement had not been undertaken in Taiwan before a surplus in the government budget and technological progress were realized. Two important factors need to be noted in this context: (a) determined government action, and (b) technological relation between the fixed capital input and biological technology. The former is related to the basic problem of capital allocation in the whole national economy. Since agriculture is generally considered the mainstay of the economy, better utilization of slack in agriculture is preferred to additional input of scarce capital funds. The latter is concerned with the availability of new varieties of seeds, with the farmers' skill in application of chemical fertilizer, and with the method of cultivation in relation to the heavy irrigation investment. The requirement for heavy irrigation investment seems to be large in the pe-

---

[1] Ishikawa, *Economic Development in Asian Perspective*, pp. 346–347; V. W. Ruttan, *Considerations in the Design of a Strategy for Increasing Rice Production in Southeast Asia*.

riod of transition from extensive to intensive farming in paddy farming areas. With the high pressure of population, there is a general tendency for labor intensive cultivation in agriculture. To absorb more labor input in farming, expansion of productive capacity in terms of land is naturally necessary. However, the intensity of farming is greatly dependent on the demand for crops and livestock as well as the quantitative and qualitative relationships between inputs. Landowners, as receivers of large shares of land rent from the additional increase of output, will play some role in encouraging such intensive farming. In Taiwan, promotion of new varieties of seeds, chemical fertilizers, and irrigation investment represented such an effort on the part of landlords.

Agricultural transformation which simultaneously maintains a net capital outflow calls for a variety of strategies. The more important of these are: (a) the basic agricultural investment should be accompanied by technological improvement; (b) an appropriate investment scheme with large labor input and less input of capital goods should be selected; and (c) a capital transfer mechanism should be established. According to the different conditions or stages of agricultural development, the above strategic components will change in relative importance, as the experience of Taiwan has shown.

When the problems of agricultural development faced by the countries currently developing in South Asia are examined, it is clear that they suffer from an inability to transform the traditional agriculture and bring about a major, continuous change in productivity associated with a technologically dynamic agriculture. The crucial fact is, as Mellor has pointed out, that introduction of single change in farming practice in such a traditional agriculture will result in only a small increase in productivity.[2] Several of the empirical studies of South Asian agriculture indicate that in a traditional agriculture, increase in agricultural production or crop yield through added labor input seems unlikely.[3] Considering the available land resources and high population pressure in the contemporary South Asian countries, the land-man ratio in these areas will continue to decrease in the future. Thus, the development strategies followed in Taiwan in 1926–1930 may prove useful for these areas. Their success will, of course, be circumscribed by the institutional and organizational framework accompanying them.

[2] Mellor, *The Economics of Agricultural Development*, pp. 214–219.
[3] Mellor, *ibid.*, pp. 136–154.

Methods and Sources for
Statistical Estimates for
Social Income Accounting
of Taiwan's Agriculture

Method of Social Income Accounting

The social income accounting method used here is constructed primarily for the purpose of measuring intersectoral capital flows. The method has two advantages: first, it is possible to check the magnitudes of commodity flows directly, and, second, the sources and usage of financial contribution from the agricultural sector to the nonagricultural sector can be investigated. In contrast to the approach of social income accounting, the national capital accounting method presents the following problems in practical measurement: (a) assessment of capital assets lacks a sound basis; and (b) when one item is in both debt and credit sides simultaneously it generally cancels itself in the capital account.

Social income accounting generally consists of three important parts: sectors, accounts, and entries (or the type of transaction). Sectors indicate the parts participating in the economic transactions of the national economy. The classification of sectors is generally made by grouping economic units which have similar types of activities. For practical purposes, the national economy of Taiwan was classified into the following sectors: agricultural production, agricultural household, nonagricultural production, nonagricultural household, public finance, and international trade. According to the basic concept of social accounting, accounting is here divided into the following items: production, expenditure, and investment. Thus, each sector has three accounts. The transactions between sectors and between accounts in the same sector become debit and credit entries of each account. As production, consumption expenditure, and investment in agriculture are generally integrated into one unit in the farm-family economic system, labor input in agricultural production is mostly derived from family labor. In addition, there are no payments for transactions of production goods, labor, or products between the farm household and the production sectors. Farmers also have some nonfarm earnings from the nonagricultural sector. The nature of agricultural production makes sectoral transactions between agricultural production and agricultural households quite complex. It is therefore difficult to separate them into two sectors. Unlike the nonagricultural sector and nonagricultural households, it is necessary to set up some fictional transactions between accounts in these sectors. This gives rise to problems of evaluation of the commodities and services in the transactions between these two sectors.

The following principles are used to solve some difficult problems which occur in the statistical procedure:

(a) Landlords are classified into three categories: part-landlords, resident landlords, and absentee landlords. Part-landlords actually participate in agricultural production and also lease some land to other cultivators. They are included in the agricultural production sector. The resident and absentee landlords are excluded from the agricultural sector for the following reasons: (1) they are generally engaged in nonagricultural economic activities; (2) they are considered as "land lenders" whose objective is earning land rent; (3) financial transactions between sectors are generally carried out in rural areas by absentee and resident landlords. Such landlords have played an important role in commercialization of agricultural products and in investment in agriculture in the early period of agricultural development. After institution of the land-reform program, the resident and absentee landlords nearly vanished, and this changed the nature of the sectoral capital outflow from the agricultural sector. Because of the original nature and function of the resident and absentee landlords and the implications of the change in the sectoral capital flow, these landlords are classified into the nonagricultural sector.

(b) Agricultural institutions, such as irrigation associations and farmers' associations, are included in the public finance or government sector. Rural cooperatives are considered as part of the nonagricultural sector. Agricultural corporations, such as those producing sugar, tea, and pineapples, are included in the agricultural production sector.

(c) Nonfarm income is considered as income produced in the nonagricultural sector, and is paid for by the supply of labor or other production services from an agricultural household. For the same reason, the family budget of the resident and absentee landlords is excluded from the agricultural household.

(d) In the agricultural household, there are no production and investment accounts. Therefore, we assume that there are no productive assets in the agricultural household and that the agricultural household fictionally rents its house and other assets from the agricultural production sector. Depreciation or appreciation of fixed assets occurs only in the agricultural production sector, so that there is neither production nor investment activity in the agricultural household sector.

(e) All commodity and service transactions between sectors are in principle valued at farm level. Wages for family labor can be imputed as a residual in the farm-production expenses.

In accordance with the above principles, a social income account for agriculture may be constructed by integrating sectors of agricultural production and agricultural household with the three accounts as follows.[1]

(1) Balance Sheet of Agricultural Production

Debit	*Credit*
a. Agricultural sector: expenditure on farm production, such as seed, feed, other agricultural materials, and depreciation.	a. Agricultural sector: same as debit side minus depreciation; incremental value of capital.
b. Nonagricultural sector: purchase of production goods, fertilizer, pesticides, feeds, agricultural implements, and other materials.	b. Nonagricultural sector: sale of agricultural products as raw materials.
c. Agricultural household sector: imputed wages for family labor and wages paid to hired labor of other farm families; imputed land-rent paid to owner-cultivators and part-landlords; imputed interest for owned capital and interest paid to other farmers.	c. Agricultural household sector: agricultural products consumed on farm household and bought from other farmers.

[1] T. H. Lee, "A Study on Structural Change of Agricultural Production in Taiwan," *Agricultural Economic Seminar Proceedings* (Taipei, Taiwan: National Taiwan University, 1958), pp. 79–89.

d. Nonagricultural household sector: land rent paid to landlords; interest paid to nonfarm money lenders.

e. Public finance: taxes collected by government and fees paid to farmers' associations and to irrigation associations.

d. Nonagricultural household sector: sale of farm products directly to nonagricultural household.

e. Public finance: subsidy from government and farmers' associations.

f. Foreign trade sector: export of agricultural goods directly to other countries.

(2) Balance Sheet of Income and Consumption

Debit

a. Agricultural sector: agricultural products consumed within agricultural households and bought from other farmers.

b. Nonagricultural sector: expenditure on nonagricultural goods.

c. Surplus to agricultural sector and nonagricultural sector as investment.

Credit

a. Agricultural sector: imputed wages for family labor, and wages received from other farmers and agricultural investment; imputed land rent paid to the owner-cultivators and part-landlords; imputed interest for owned capital and interest paid by other farmers.

b. Nonagricultural sector: wages from nonagricultural sector; property revenue from nonagricultural sector; interest for farmers' investment in nonagricultural sector.

c. Statistical discrepancy.

(3) Balance Sheet of Savings and Investment

Debit	Credit
a. Agricultural sector: incremental value of plant, animals, and inventories.	a. Agricultural sector: depreciation.
b. Agricultural household sector: wage paid to labor input in investment.	b. Agricultural household sector: surplus transferred from the agricultural household sector for investment.
c. Nonagricultural sector: purchase of capital goods from nonagriculture.	c. Nonagricultural sector: investment made by landlord and borrowed from financial institutions.
	d. Public finance sector: government and farmers' associations' investments in the agricultural sector.

Sources of Information for Statistical Estimates

The statistical estimates used here for social income accounting for Taiwan's agriculture were made for the periods 1911–1940 and 1950–1960. For the period 1895–1911 statistical information is not available for a serial estimate. Taiwan then was in the initial stage of development during which several important social and economic reforms were imposed by Japanese authorities; these were subsequently followed by a continuous flow of technological innovations from Japan. This period is so important in Taiwan's agricultural transformation from long-term stagnation that we have tried to quote (in Chapter 3) some fragmentary data in order to make an indirect comparison. In contrast to the relative shortage of statistics during 1895–1911, most of the statistics published by the government during the war and the postwar period, 1940–1950, were manipulated or voided for reasons of national security, and, since rapid inflation in the postwar period made valuation of commodity and service transactions between two sectors extremely difficult, the estimates for the period 1941–1949 were excluded from consideration.

The following government statistics and survey reports constituted the major statistical sources: (a) the farm economic survey for rice-producing farmers in 1925 and in 1931–1932 which covered fifty sample farmers each; the farm-family expenditure survey for rice-producing farmers in 1936–1937 which had 189 samples; and the farm economic survey in 1950–1951 which covered 281 farm families' records (the farm income survey and the farm record program have been conducted for 200 farm families every year since 1954) ; (b) production cost surveys of major crops such as rice, sugar cane, tea, peanuts, and jute; these have been conducted every fifth year since 1925; (c) an agricultural yearbook for Taiwan, published every year since 1901, which includes data on production of crops and livestock, utilization of fertilizer, area and number of various large trees, area of farm land, farm implements, and agricultural prices.

Procedure for Statistical Estimates for Balance Sheets

(1) BALANCE SHEET OF AGRICULTURAL PRODUCTION

Agricultural Sector in Credit Column (a) and Debit Column (a). This account includes the value of farm products used on the farm as intermediate goods, such as seed, feed, small trees, miscellaneous materials, and depreciation. On the credit side of this account, the incremental value of animals and woodlands takes the place of depreciation in the debit side. The total value of seed is obtained through the total individual seed costs for seventy-six crops, calculated by multiplying average seed quantity per hectare by total crop area and by average annual current price of that crop. The average quantity of seed per hectare is quoted from various sources, such as cost survey data, agronomy data from experimental stations, and the special report of crop production made by government and individual research surveys. A long series of cost data could be obtained from various sources for main crops, such as rice, sugar cane, and sweet potato, and an incomplete series for minor crops and livestock.[2] Total feed cost is obtained from the sum of the total feed cost for the individual animals and birds. The total feed cost of individual items is estimated by multiplying average feed consumption of sweet potato, sweet potato vine, and vegetables each per head by its midyear number and by current average annual prices of feed products. The seedling and small trees are estimated in the same way as is the seed cost. Depreciation on farm buildings and implements was estimated through the expansion of per hectare depreciation reported by the rice production cost survey. Total farm land area is used as the basis for this simple expansion. Incremental value of capital is obtained from the previous study on farm assets estimated by the Rural Economics Division of the Joint Commission on Rural Reconstruction through the period 1910–1960.[3]

Nonagricultural Sector in Credit Column (b). Sale of agricultural products to processing industries and livestock slaughtered are included in this account. Most of the data

[2] S. C. Hsieh and T. H. Lee, "An Analytical Review of Agricultural Development in Taiwan—An Input-Output and Productivity Approach," *op. cit.*, pp. 21–23, Appendix 2 & 3.

[3] United Nations, Economic Commission for Asia and Far East, "Relationship between Agriculture and Industrial Development: A Case Study in Taiwan," *Economic Bulletin for Asia and Far East*, Vol. 14, No. 1 (June 1963), pp. 58–59.

is quoted from our previous study on utilization of farm products and livestock.[4] This study includes a comprehensive investigation of production and raw material requirements reported by processing industries every year. Total number of livestock slaughtered is reported by town and city offices to the Provincial Department of Agriculture and Forestry through their collection of the slaughtering tax. A long trend of slaughtering ratio is also used to check the possible omission of livestock slaughtered by exemption of tax and by illegal slaughtering. Valuation of those crops and livestock are made at the farm level of average annual prices.

Nonagricultural Sector in Debit Column (b). Purchase of nonagricultural production goods, such as fertilizers, pesticides, other chemicals, farm machinery, feed and miscellaneous materials, is included in this account. Total value of chemical fertilizer consumption is obtained from the Taiwan Agricultural Yearbook and from the fertilizer manual published by the Provincial Food Bureau. These figures have been checked against domestic production, import quantity, and carry-over, and lastly, adjusted to the farm price level. Some organic fertilizer such as soybean cake and fishbone are also included in this item.[5] Statistics on pesticides and chemical consumption are based on the report of pesticides and chemical production and import estimated by the Joint Commission on Rural Reconstruction annually. Total purchase of farm machinery and implements is estimated from statistics of industrial production and foreign trade.[6] The agricul-

[4] "Utilization of Agricultural Products," unpublished report (Taipei, Taiwan: Joint Commission on Rural Reconstruction, Rural Economics Division), estimated tables.

[5] *Taiwan Agricultural Yearbook*, annual issues.

[6] Taiwan Provincial Government, *T'aiwan wu-shih-i nien lai t'ung chi* (in Chinese) [The Fifty-one Years' Statistics] (Taipei, Taiwan, 1946).

tural censuses of 1955 and 1960 have been used to check the ratio between quantity of farmers' purchase and quantity of production and import over a long period. A limited amount of farm economy survey data has also been used for reference.[7] Consumption of purchased feed mostly consists of soybean cake and peanut cake. Some of these cakes were applied as fertilizer in the early period, and detailed estimates of both types of consumption have been made by fertilizer and livestock specialists in the "Fertilizer Problem in Taiwan" and "Livestock of Taiwan" published by the Bank of Taiwan. The detailed report of fertilizer distribution in the postwar period is published in "Taiwan Agricultural Yearbook" by the Provincial Department of Agriculture and Forestry, and the "Taiwan Food Statistics Book" of the Provincial Food Bureau. After deduction of soybean cake and other cakes used for fertilizer from total consumption, the remaining quantity is estimated as feeds. The production cost surveys of hogs which were undertaken by the Taiwan Governor General's Office and the Provincial Department of Agriculture and Forestry in 1935 and 1951 give a detailed analysis of the consumption of different feeds by hogs in different types of farming areas. Data from these surveys have been used as key figures in checking the above statistics of total feed consumption and the quantity of feeds purchased by farmers. Miscellaneous materials include spare parts for farm machinery and implements, fuel, materials for house repair, and similar small items. The estimate of these expenses is completely based on "Rice Production Cost Survey" of the Provincial Food Bureau for the period since 1936. Before 1936 an incomplete survey of rice production cost, conducted

[7] Taiwan Agricultural Census Committee, *Report on the 1956 Sample Census of Agriculture,* August 1959; also, *Taiwan Agricultural Census Report for 1960,* Vol. 1, 1961.

every five years, was used. The estimate is made by multiplying per hectare miscellaneous expenses by the total farmland area. Since it includes so many different small items and since the estimate is based on a value unit, the reliability of these estimated figures is doubtful. If the estimate is compared with the per hectare average figures reported in the farm economic survey, some underestimation is observed in our statistics. But the increasing trend of expenses closely corresponds to the farm economic survey data.

Agricultural Household Sector in Credit Column (c). Consumption of agricultural products by agricultural households is recorded in this account which includes also the purchases of agricultural products between farmers. Estimate of farmers' self-consumption is obtained from study on "Utilization of Agricultural Products" and "Food Balance Sheet of Taiwan" published by the Joint Commission on Rural Reconstruction.[8] The survey on "Farmers' Sale and Consumption of Agricultural Products" undertaken in 1930 and "Farmers' Purchase and Sale of Farm and Industrial Products" conducted jointly by the Provincial Food Bureau and the Joint Commission on Rural Reconstruction in 1962 are most useful for ascertaining per capita consumption of individual farm products by farmers and urban population. The basic data estimated in "Utilization of Agricultural Products" were obtained by estimating utilization of individual products through marketing channels. The total self-consumption of farm products on the farm was estimated with the use of figures on per capita consumption and total agricultural population. In this estimate agricultural products provided through processing or slaughtering are not

[8] "Food Balance Sheet of Taiwan" (Taipei, Taiwan: Joint Commission on Rural Reconstruction, Rural Economics Division), annual issues, 1935–1960.

accounted as self-consumption. Therefore a great number of farm products acquired through processing are omitted from this account and recorded in the nonagricultural sector in the balance sheet of income and consumption.

Agricultural Household Sector in Debit Column (c). Estimates of the entries in this account are quite different from other accounts. As family labor, capital, and owned land are not actually paid for their contribution in production, some different imputation methods are adopted for family labor and other production factors. Interest on capital and land rent of owned land were based on the interest rate actually paid by farmers to other sectors and the average per hectare land rent actually paid to a landlord for paddy land and dry land respectively. Total farm assets minus liability are considered as owned capital which is estimated from the farm assets estimate. Revolving capital which was used for payment of wages and purchase of production goods is estimated from an earlier input-output and productivity study on agricultural development in Taiwan.[9] From the above fixed and current capital, total interest was computed by current average annual interest rate reported by the Bank of Taiwan. The same method is also applied to the estimate of total land rent. Land rent which has to be imputed to the agricultural sector is based on different categories of farm, paddy, and dry land, which are actually owned by farmers. The remaining amount of land rent (subtracting the above land rent for farmers from total land rent) is imputed to the resident and absentee landlords in the nonagricultural sector. Wages paid to hired labor and family labor were computed separately. Wages actually paid to hired labor by other

[9] S. C. Hsieh and T. H. Lee, "An Analytical Review of Agricultural Development in Taiwan—An Input-Output and Productivity Approach," *op. cit.*, p. 38, Appendix Table 4.

farmers are estimated by multiplying current wage per day by total hired labor days. The estimate of total hired labor days is used from the input-output and productivity study.[10] This was estimated from the labor hired for producing each individual crop as reported in the crop production cost surveys. Total working days of family labor are also estimated from the crop production cost surveys and the livestock production cost survey, but total return to family labor is computed as the residual of total net agricultural income by subtracting wages paid, interest paid and imputed, and land rent paid and imputed. Viewed from the specific nature of family farming, return to family labor should not be valued at current wage rate, but should rather be computed as the residual of net farm income.

Nonagricultural Household Sector in Credit Column (d). This account includes the total sale of agricultural products directly to households in the nonagricultural sector. The sources of information to estimate the total sale in this account are almost the same as those in farm consumption of agricultural products.

Nonagricultural Household Sector in Debit Column (d). This account includes interest and land rent paid to the nonagricultural households covering resident and absentee landlords, moneylenders, and financial institutions. The estimate method of this account was previously described in the agricultural household sector in debit side.

Public Finance in Credit Column (e). This account includes subsidies provided by the government and farmers' associations to farmers to encourage production or adoption of new techniques. The government expenditures on agricultural experiments and extension were not included in this

[10] S. C. Hsieh and T. H. Lee, *ibid.*

account. In the postwar period, the government collected rice and other crops at official prices. The government payment for rice purchase is also included in this account. The differences between the official prices and prices at farm level are accounted as hidden taxes and recorded in the debit side. The quantity of government purchase is limited only to the compulsory portion, and barter exchange is not accounted here.[11]

Public Finance in Debit Column (*e*). Included in this account are: land tax, household tax, agricultural income tax, house tax, car license tax, defense tax, and surtax on the above tax items, fees for farmers' associations, water fees, and hidden tax through collection and barter exchange of farm products at low official prices. Government budget statistics including provincial, prefecture, and township offices, the tax report, the unpublished financial report of rice and other crops collected by the Provincial Food Bureau, and the annual report of the Joint Commission on Rural Reconstruction were the main sources of information for the estimate of this account.[12] To estimate the tax burden shared by the agricultural sector, the following methods are adopted for our estimate. Since land tax is separated into city tax and farm land tax of paddy and dry land in the government

[11] Taiwan Provincial Food Bureau, *T'aiwan liang shih yao lan* (in Chinese) [Taiwan Food Statistics Book], Taipei, Taiwan, annual editions, 1946–1960, pp. 271–272.

[12] Taiwan Provincial Bureau of Accounts and Statistics, *Taiwan Statistical Abstract,* 1950–1960 annual issue, p. 181; Taiwan Provincial Department of Finance, *T'aiwan t'sai-cheng t'ung-chi nien pao* (in Chinese [Finance Statistics of Taiwan] (Taipei, Taiwan: annual issue 1946–1960), pp. 10–20; C. Y. Hsu, "Rural Taxation in Taiwan" (Taipei, Taiwan: Joint Commission on Rural Reconstruction, unpublished mimeograph, 1952), pp. 1–25.

budget, the household tax paid by agriculture is estimated by total household tax collected by prefecture and township offices (excluding the amount of household tax collected by city government) multiplied by the ratio of the number of farm households to the total number of households in the districts of prefecture and township offices. House tax is also estimated by the same method. Income tax paid by the agricultural sector is obtained by multiplying total income tax collection in city, prefecture, and township offices by the ratio of agricultural income to total national income. This item had no importance in the prewar period, because there was no tax on farmers' income. Car license tax which is usually charged on oxcarts and bicycles, is estimated by the ratio of oxcarts and bicycles owned by farmers to the total number of those cars. Defense and surtaxes generally are imposed on every tax at a given rate. Therefore, we estimated the total defense and surtax paid by agriculture by multiplying a given rate of taxing by the total amount of taxes on above items paid by agriculture. Farmers' association fees and water fees are directly quoted from the annual report of farmers' and irrigation associations or the annual report of the Provincial Water Conservation Bureau.

Foreign Trade Sector (*f*). Only direct export of agricultural products is indicated in this account. Exports of processed or manufactured agricultural products are excluded from this item. Imports of industrial goods and agricultural commodities are not considered to be direct transactions between agricultural production and foreign trade. Consumption of imported capital goods by agriculture is considered as purchased by the agricultural sector from the nonagricultural sector. Prices used for valuation of total exports are fixed at farm level.

(2) BALANCE SHEET OF INCOME AND CONSUMPTION

Agricultural Sector in Credit Column (a). This account includes an entry from the agricultural household sector in the balance sheet of agricultural production and labor income in agricultural investment, indicating income of farm household derived from agriculture.

Agricultural Sector in Debit Column (a). This account is identical with the account of the agricultural household sector in the balance sheet of agricultural production.

Nonagricultural Sector in Credit Column (b). This indicates the items of farmers' income from the nonagricultural sector covering wages and property income and business revenue received from the economic activities of farmers in the nonagricultural sector. In this estimate this item was the most difficult one because of the scarcity of available data. The percentage of nonagricultural income in total farm family income reported in the "Farm Economic Survey" is considered as only one source for estimating nonfarm income. However, as previously mentioned, the farm economic survey was conducted only on a small scale in the prewar period. Their data are not enough to cover the changes in nonfarm income from time to time. It was considered more convenient to estimate this account as a residual of transactions between accounts in the production, consumption, and investment balance tables. In view of the cash balance in the balancing of farm economy, this estimation is not very far from reality. Thus, statistical discrepancy between the three balance tables is also included in this account. Through our comparison of the estimated amount with the nonfarm income reported in the "Farm Economic Survey," a similar trend is found in the two series. Roughly speaking, the percentage of nonfarm income in total farm family income has increased through time. In the original farm economic survey, nonfarm income means income received from outside farm work and economic activities in the nonagricultural sector. Therefore, it includes income from both sectors, agriculture and nonagriculture. Only income from the nonagricultural sector is taken into consideration in our case. The above comparison of the two series then is based on the adjusted nonfarm income in the "Farm Economic Survey."

Nonagricultural Sector in Debit Column (*b*). Purchase of consumer goods from the nonagricultural sector is recorded in this account. Processed agricultural goods are undoubtedly considered as entries in this account. The estimate of this account is based on the linear relationship between per capita agricultural household consumption and per capita agricultural net income. The per capita self-consumption of agricultural products is then subtracted from per capita total agricultural consumption. The linear relationship between per capita agricultural net income and per capita consumption is made by two series of estimated per capita agricultural income and per capita consumption reported in the "Farm Economic Survey" conducted in 1925, 1931–1932, 1936–1937, and 1950–1960. Per capita consumption of nonagricultural goods thus obtained is expanded by total population in agriculture to get total consumption of nonagricultural goods in the agricultural sector.

Surplus to Agricultural Sector and Nonagricultural Sector (*c*). This is the balance between income and consumption of agricultural households which will be appropriated into agricultural and nonagricultural investment. The former is the entry from the "Balance Sheet of Saving and Investment." Nonagricultural investment includes deposits in banks and rural credit cooperatives as well as the purchase of bonds and stocks in industrial enterprises. The estimate of nonagricultural investment is based on the annual reports of rural credit cooperatives and capital accounting in the farm economic survey data. In reference to changes in capital stock and deposits of rural credit cooperatives, a detailed analysis of sources of those funds has been reported in the annual reports of the rural credit cooperatives. Landlords, businessmen, owner cultivators, and tenants are the main categories for this classification. Contribution of capital from agriculture to rural credit cooperatives is estimated through these annual reports. Other types of capital transfer are estimated from the farm economic survey and the farmers' financial survey.[13]

(3) BALANCE SHEET OF SAVINGS AND INVESTMENT

Agricultural Sector in Credit and Debit Columns (a). Entry of this account on the credit side is the depreciation which can be posted from the agricultural sector in the debit side. The debit side demonstrates the same situation.

Agricultural Household Sector in Debit and Credit Columns (b). The credit account here is posted from surplus to the agricultural sector in the debit side. Wages paid to farmers for their labor input in agricultural investment are recorded in this account.

Nonagricultural Sector in Credit Column (c). Investments made by landlords and funds borrowed from financial institutions are included in this account. Since irrigation investment cost is generally to be shared by landlords, their

[13] Cooperative Bank of Taiwan, *Ho-tso t'ung-chi nien-pao* (in Chinese) [Annual Statistics of Credit Cooperatives] annual issue, pp. 94–125; Taiwan Governor General's Office, *Nōgyō kinyū chōsa hōkoku* (in Japanese) [The Report on Agricultural Credit], 1933, pp. 1–80; Taiwan Provincial Department of Agriculture and Forestry, *Nung-yeh shin yon t'iao cha* (in Chinese) [*Report on Agricultural Credit,*] 1950, 1951, and 1960 issues pp. 1–105.

contribution is estimated by ratio of land area owned by absentee landlords to total farmland area. Investment funds borrowed from financial institutions are estimated from annual reports of rural credit cooperatives, the land bank, and the cooperative bank. Intermediate and long-term agricultural loans made by those financial agencies are quoted as investment funds from nonagriculture.

Nonagricultural Sector in Debit Column (c). Purchase of capital goods is included in this account. Estimate of capital goods input in investment is made separately by type of investment, such as irrigation, house construction, machinery, and land reclamation. The ratio of capital goods input in per unit agricultural investment has been estimated by the engineers in "Irrigation Problems in Taiwan."[14] Those ratios were applied to the estimate of the amounts of labor input and capital goods input in the total agricultural investment.

Public Finance Sector in Credit Column (d). The amount of agricultural investment made by the government, farmers' associations, and the Joint Commission on Rural Reconstruction is entered in this account. Estimation of their investment is based on the government's annual budget, and the annual reports of farmers' associations and the Joint Commission on Rural Reconstruction.

The outline shows the statistical procedure followed for constructing social income accounting of agriculture. The estimation of intersectoral net capital transfer in the period 1895–1910 is based only on some major statistics, which include factor price payment, government taxing, and financial transactions.

[14] *T'aiwan ti shui-li* (in Chinese) [Irrigation Problems in Taiwan], *T'aiwan yen-chiu ts'ung kan* (in Chinese) [Special Series No. 4] (Taipei, Taiwan, 1950), p. 95.

The terms of trade are considered as the ratio of prices received and paid by farmers at farm level. To analyze the effect of changes in the terms of trade on net real capital transfer, two price indices were computed with the following procedure. The price index of farmers' receipt was calculated by using average production quantity in 1935–1937 as the weight.[15] Marketable agricultural products were selected for this computation. This price series was computed first in 1958 and has been revised several times for the purposes of this study. The index of prices paid by farmers has been computed for 32 items by the Joint Commission on Rural Reconstruction and Provincial Government since 1950 and has been published since 1952.[16] During this period a revision of the list of items and of the weight- and price-reporting system has been made twice. However, some agricultural commodities such as rice, sweet potatoes, and other important goods are also included in the items of the price index paid by farmers. This makes the index of prices paid biased and parallel to the index of prices received by farmers. No method exists at present to correct such statistical bias in the series for the postwar period. For the prewar period, a new series of prices paid by farmers was constructed by the following method. Six items of commodities for production and seven items for living expenditure were selected for computation with the percentage of farmers' expenditure on those commodities in total expenditure in 1935–1937. Prices of those commodities at farm level are not avail-

[15] S. C. Hsieh and T. H. Lee, "Agricultural Development and Its Contributions to Economic Growth in Taiwan," *op. cit.*, pp. 36–37.

[16] Taiwan Provincial Bureau of Accounts and Statistics, *T'aiwan nung-ming so-teh so-fu chia-keh chih shu* (in Chinese) [Indices of Prices Received and Paid by Farmers] (Taipei, Taiwan, monthly issue, 1950–1960), pp. 12–14.

able. Therefore, wholesale prices were used for computing the trend in each commodity price. To connect these two series of the prewar and postwar price indices paid by farmers, 1952 and 1937 were selected as connecting points. There is no significant difference in the results obtained. The terms of trade thus computed were compared with the old price ratio between the price index received by farmers and the general price index which has been used for the time. The result shows that there are no great upward or downward discrepancies in the trend between the two indices.

APPENDIX B

Population Growth and Economic Development

The following studies deal with the impact of population growth on economic development: D. W. Jorgenson, "The Development of Dual Economy," *Economic Journal* (June 1961), pp. 309–311; John C. H. Fei and Gustav Ranis, "Agrarianism, Dualism, and Economic Development," in Irma Adelman and Eric Thorbecke, eds., *The Theory and Design of Economic Development* (Baltimore: Johns Hopkins Press, 1966), pp. 7–23; Ryoshin Minami, "Keizai Seicho no Koten Gakuha Teki Setsukin ni Tsuiite" (in Japanese) [Classical Approach to Economic Growth], *Keizai Kenkyu* (in Japanese) [The Economic Review], Hitotsubashi University, July 1965. The author is indebted to Minami's paper for derivation of the conditional equation in the text.

Whether the economy can escape from the Malthusian trap or will fall into it depends on the rate of technological change. Two stages of economic growth can be assumed to correspond to these situations with two possible population response curves. In stage one, population is considered as an endogenous variable, and in stage two it is considered as an exogenous variable. They can be expressed as:

$$G(\mathcal{N}) = a(W - \hat{W}) \quad \text{(stage one)} \tag{1}$$
$$G(\mathcal{N}) = r \quad \text{(stage two)}$$

In stage one, population growth is dependent on change in the living standard or wage rate. If the wage rate (W) is larger than the subsistence wage level $(\hat{W})$, population then will increase through the decrease in death rate. In stage two, population growth is dependent on the change of natural birth rate. To classify these two stages, a given wage rate corresponding to the maximum natural birth rate can be conceived as the turning point. When we indicate the wage rate at this turning point as $\overset{*}{W}$, the long-run equilibrium wage rate $(\bar{W})$ can be located in the region below $(\overset{*}{W})$ in the case of stage one, and in the upper region $(\overset{*}{W})$ in the case of stage two. The above population response curve can be shown in the following figure.

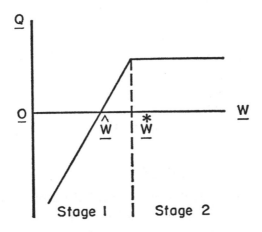

In this illustration, $\overset{*}{W}$ at turning point thus can be defined from equations (1) as,

$$\overset{*}{W} = \frac{r}{a} + \hat{W} \qquad (2)$$

where a is the slope of the population response curve. If the long-run equilibrium wage level (W) is located between $\hat{W}$ and W the initial wage rate (W) will monotonically approach the point $(\bar{W})$ of the long-run wage rate by the assumption of a population response curve. The economy will stagnate in the Malthusian trap. When the long-run wage rate lies in the upper region $(\overset{*}{W})$, the initial wage rate (W) will approach this long-run wage rate even if it is located below the turning point (W). In this case, the economy can shift from stage one to stage two.

To derive the conditional equation for the shift of economy from stage one to stage two, we will make an investigation of the conditions for stage two in which the long-run wage rate $(\overline{W})$ is given in the region above the turning point $(\overset{*}{W})$. The production function is assumed to be of the Cobb-Douglass form, including output (Y), the production factors of capital (K), labor (N), and land (D). Constant returns to scale and the law of diminishing return to factors are still held in this case. The production function thus can be expressed as:

$$Y = F(K, N, D, t) \tag{3}$$

The dynamic production function thus can be derived in the following way:

$$y = g + \alpha n + \beta k + \gamma d \tag{3}'$$

In this instance y is the growth rate of output, g the neutral technological change, n, k, and d the growth rates of labor, capital, and land respectively; α, β, and γ are the production elasticities of labor, capital, and land respectively. Constant returns to scale and the diminishing returns to production factors are assumed. The goal of production is to seek a high profit rate under the restriction of equation (3). The equilibrium condition for maximizing profit rate in the static case is

$$i = \beta \frac{Y}{K} = \frac{\delta Y}{\delta K} \tag{4}$$

Wage rate is determined as follows:

$$W = \alpha \frac{Y}{N} = \frac{\delta Y}{\delta N} \tag{5}$$

Equations (4) and (5) mean that profit rate and wage rate at the equilibrium point are equal to the marginal productivity of capital and marginal productivity of labor. For simplification, we assume that α, β and γ are constant. Then the growth rates of wage rate and interest rate will be:

$$G(W) = y - n \tag{6}$$
$$G(i) = y - k \tag{7}$$

If total profit is saved for investment, capital investment ceases at the point of interest rate $(\hat{\imath})$. The average propensity to save or saving ratio is defined as s; then the growth rate of capital stock can be shown as:

$$G(K) = s(i - \hat{\imath}) = k \tag{8}$$

Cultivated land is assumed constant, then $D = \bar{D}$ and

$$G(D) = 0 \tag{9}$$

From the above equations, equation (3)' can be expressed as

$$G(i) = g + \alpha r - s(i - \hat{\imath})(1 - \beta) \tag{10}$$

where r is the natural growth rate of population. To obtain the long-run equilibrium interest rate $(\bar{\imath})$, solve equation (10) by putting $G(i) = 0$. Then we have

$$\bar{\imath} = \frac{g + \alpha r}{s(1 - \beta)} + \hat{\imath} \tag{11}$$

Substituting this into equation (10), it will be

$$G(i) = s(1 - \beta)(\bar{\imath} - i) \tag{12}$$

As term $(1 - \beta)$ is positive, $G(i)$ is stable. From equations (11) and (12), it should be clear that $G(Y) = G(K)$. $G(K)$ can be shown as

$$G(K) = G(Y) = \frac{g + \alpha r}{1 - \beta} \tag{13}$$

By reducing r from equation (13) we can obtain

$$G(W) = G\left(\frac{Y}{N}\right) = \frac{g - (1 - \alpha - \beta)r}{1 - \beta} = \frac{g - \gamma r}{1 - \beta} \tag{14}$$

From equation (14), population increases in relation to different stages of economic development can be specified as follows:

$$G(W) = G\left(\frac{K}{N}\right) = G\left(\frac{Y}{N}\right) \gtreqless 0 \text{ when } r \lesseqgtr \frac{g}{\gamma} \tag{15}$$

Equation (15) indicates that the growth rate of real wage rate will be positive (>0), zero ($= 0$), or negative (<0), if the population growth rate (r) is smaller than, equal to or larger than ($\lesseqgtr$) technological change rate (g) dividing by the production elasticity of land (γ). Therefore, the positive growth rate of real wage rate is dependent on the higher technological change rate and intensive land use. The national economy thus can move from the first stage to the second stage.

To adjust the above conditional equation (15) to the real situation in agriculture, the following modification will be necessary:

$$r \gtreqless \frac{g}{\gamma} + \theta \tag{16}$$

where θ is the growth rate of the cropland area.

 APPENDIX C

Biased Efficiency Growth
and Production Function

We assume initially that the aggregate production is a homogeneous function of the first degree in inputs of capital and labor measured in efficiency terms and that it has a constant elasticity of substitution between the inputs. Thus, we have

$$V = [(E_L L)^{-e} + (E_K K)^{-e}]^{-\frac{1}{e}} \qquad (1)[1]$$

where $\rho = \dfrac{1 - \sigma}{\sigma} \geq -1$, σ is the elasticity of substitution between K and L and that fulfills the above requirements and also obeys the normal conditions for the production function in relation to the first and second derivatives with respect to output (V). In our analysis, the notations V, L, and K represent output per hectare of land, per hectare labor input in working days, and capital stock per hectare, respectively. The coefficients E_L and E_K then represent the level of efficiency of the conventional inputs of labor (measured in working days) and capital (measured in irrigation facilities, cattle, agricultural tools, and orchard trees). Vanek has de-

---

[1] P. A. David and T. H. Vard de Klundert, "Biased Efficiency Growth and Capital-Labor Substitution in the United States, 1899–1960," *American Economic Review*, Vol. 55 (June 1965), pp. 359–394.

fined such a production function in the following generalized type.[2]

$$Y = F(e^{at}N, e^{bt}K) \tag{2}$$

in which a and b express the increase in efficiency of labor and capital at exponential rate through time.

For statistical measurement, the set of equivalences of equation (1) can be derived by partially differentiating it with respect to L and K first, and then differentiating equation (1) and marginal productivity of labor and capital each with respect to time. Substituting the growth equation of marginal productivity of labor and capital into the growth equation of net output, we obtain:[3]

$$\frac{\dot{V}}{V} = \alpha \left(\frac{\dot{L}}{L} + \frac{\dot{E}_L}{E_L} \right) + \beta \left(\frac{\dot{K}}{K} + \frac{\dot{E}_K}{E_K} \right) \tag{3}$$

where α and β represent the elasticity of production or share of income with respect to L and K. This is the modified equation of the CES model developed by Arrow, Chenery, Minhas, and Solow. Immediately, it is clear that technical coefficient $\dot{F}/F$ in the CES model is now separated in our equation as follows:

[2] J. Vanek, "Toward a More General Theory of Growth with Technological Change," *Economic Journal* (December 1965), pp. 641–654.

[3] If the equation (1) is partially differentiated with respect to L and K, it yields:

$$\frac{\delta V}{\delta L} = E_L{}^{-\rho} \left(\frac{V}{L} \right)^{1+\rho} \tag{2$'$}$$

$$\frac{\delta V}{\delta K} = E_K{}^{-\rho} \left(\frac{V}{K} \right)^{1+\rho} \tag{3$'$}$$

Now, if (1), (2)$'$ and (3)$'$ are differentiated with respect to time, we obtain:

$$\frac{\dot{V}}{V} = \alpha \left(\frac{\dot{L}}{L} + \frac{\dot{E}_L}{E_L} \right) + \beta \left(\frac{\dot{K}}{K} + \frac{\dot{E}_K}{E_K} \right) \tag{4$'$}$$

$$\frac{\dot{F}}{F} = \alpha \left(\frac{\dot{E}_L}{E_L}\right) + \beta \left(\frac{\dot{E}_K}{E_K}\right) \tag{4}$$

This indicates that technical change can be interpreted as a concept of factor efficiency or factor-augmenting technical change. Vanek has categorized this type of technical innovation by designating the inequality between $\dot{E}_L/E_L$ and $\dot{E}_K/E_K$ under the different cases of elasticity of substitution $(\sigma \gtreqless 1)$.[4]

If we divide equation $(2)'$ in the footnote by the wage rate (W), and rearrange the terms, we have:

$$\alpha = E_L{}^{\sigma-1}W^{1-\sigma} \tag{5}$$

Assuming that the efficiency of conventional labor input grows through time at the exponential rate λ_L, then equation (5) will be

$$\alpha = E_L(0)e^{\lambda_L(\sigma-1)t}W^{1-\sigma} \tag{6}$$

In a natural logarithmic expression, equation (4) can immediately be shown in equation (5), by which the parameter σ and λ_L may be estimated without any information about the growth of conventional capital inputs:

$$ln\alpha = lnE_L(0) + (1-\sigma)lnW + \lambda_L(\sigma-1)t \tag{7}$$

To estimate the efficiency of conventional capital input, equation (3) can be used for direct computation with the information of growth contained in V, L, and K.

We tried to make equation (7) by least-square regression express the substitution between labor and capital and the

---

[4] J. Vanek, *ibid.*, pp. 644. He sums up the analysis as follows:

	$a - b > 0$	$a - b < 0$
$\sigma > 1$	*c.s.*	*l.s.*
$\sigma < 1$	*l.s.*	*c.s.*

where *c.s.* and *l.s.* stand for technical innovation of capital and labor saving respectively, and σ is defined as elasticity of substitution.

efficiency of factor inputs in increasing land productivity in three periods. The statistical measurement yielded the following results:

For the period 1911–1926:

$$ln\alpha = 1.05178 \quad + 0.356369 lnW - 0.006654t$$

$$\begin{array}{ccc} & (1.0481) & (1.331) \quad R = 0.81 \\ & P = 0.2 & P = 0.1 \end{array}$$

For the period 1926–1940:

$$ln\alpha = 0.663579 + 0.52096 lnW + 0.00033t$$

$$\begin{array}{ccc} & (1.7253) & (-0.638) \quad R = 0.887 \\ & P = 0.1 & P = 0.25 \end{array}$$

For the period of 1950–1960:

$$ln\alpha = 0.58297 \quad + 0.5861 lnW - 0.0043t$$

$$\begin{array}{ccc} & (2.315) & (-0.756) \quad R = 0.929 \\ & P = 0.025 & P = 0.25 \end{array}$$

The figures appearing in parentheses under the regression coefficients are t-values derived from the tests of null-hypothesis. The respective coefficients are significantly different from zero at the different probability levels as shown below the t-value.

 APPENDIX D

Exports of Agricultural
Products and Capital Transfer

This section deals with the growth of agricultural exports
and their relevance to agriculture's contribution to the overall development of the economy.

Trade in the Colonial Period 1895–1945

Japan's administration of Taiwan prompted economic
transformation as mentioned in Chapter 3. Economic and
political features of the two areas are so closely related that
it is difficult to conceive of trade between Taiwan and Japan
as international. Tariff, exchange rate, and settlement of
foreign exchange, for example, did not exist between them.
About 16 percent of the total supply of rice and more than
80 percent of the total supply of sugar in the Japanese market
came from Taiwan. Such undifferentiated trade between the
two areas greatly affected economic growth in Japan by sta-
bilizing food prices, by meeting the foreign exchange gap,
and by contributing to capital accumulation.[1] Taiwan also
benefited from the inflow of capital goods, chemical fertilizers, and industrial production materials. The gains from
trade were primarily a result of the comparative advantages
derived from Taiwan's specialization in food production and
Japan's in manufacturing. The evidence shows that in Japan

[1] Kamekichi Takahashi, *Modern Taiwan Economy*, pp. 309–316.

the supply of food could not keep up with the demand and that a great quantity of rice was imported from Korea and Taiwan after 1918.[2] As shown below in Table 26, the net

Table 26. Food balance sheet of Taiwan, 1911–1960
(in T$millions at 1935–1937 value)

Period	(1) Total supply of food	(2) Domestic food consumption	(3) Net export of food	(4) Col. (3) as % of Col. (1)
1911–1915	158	133	25	16
1916–1920	183	146	37	20
1921–1925	217	167	49	23
1926–1930	271	196	75	29
1931–1935	333	208	125	38
1936–1940	374	219	155	42
1941–1945	297	222	75	25
1946–1950	291	269	22	8
1951–1955	430	405	25	6
1956–1960	534	505	29	5

Source: S. C. Hsieh and T. H. Lee, "Agricultural Development and Its Contributions to Economic Growth in Taiwan" (Taipei, Taiwan: Joint Commission on Rural Reconstruction, April 1966), p. 90.

export of food from Taiwan increased quite rapidly up to 1940.

To obtain a clear picture of the rapid increase in the total exports to Japan, the exports are divided into two parts; exports to Japan and exports to other areas. Table 27 indicates clearly that expansion of Taiwanese exports and imports was largely due to the rapid increase in trade between Taiwan and Japan. The trade volume between Taiwan and Japan was only 19 percent of Taiwan's total trade in 1898, but it rapidly increased to 73 percent in 1913 and then to 91 percent in 1938.

[2] Kazushi Ohkawa and Henry Rosovsky, "The Role of Agriculture in Modern Japanese Economic Development," op. cit., pp. 55–56.

Table 27. Exports and imports of Taiwan, 1898–1938 (in T$millions at current value)

Period	(1) Japan			(2) Other areas			Total trade balance	Percentage of trade with Japan in the total trade $\frac{(1)}{(1)+(2)}$
	Export	Import	Balance	Export	Import	Balance		
1898	2.1	3.7	Δ 1.6*	12.8	12.7	0.1	Δ 1.5	19
1903	9.7	11.2	Δ 1.5	11.0	11.0	Δ †	Δ 1.5	49
1908	24.4	20.4	4.0	9.3	17.1	Δ 7.8	Δ 3.8	63
1913	40.4	42.8	Δ 2.4	12.9	18.0	Δ 5.1	Δ 7.5	73
1918	106.0	70.7	35.3	33.4	33.6	Δ 0.2	35.1	73
1923	169.4	71.0	98.4	29.2	39.1	Δ10.0	88.5	78
1928	214.5	132.3	82.2	33.9	58.3	Δ24.4	57.8	79
1933	230.7	149.9	80.8	17.7	35.5	Δ17.8	63.0	88
1938	420.1	327.6	92.5	36.4	38.7	Δ 2.4	90.1	91

* Δ = import surplus
† Actual figure = T$22,000
Source: "Statistics of Taiwan's International Trade for 53 Years," Taiwan Provincial Government, Bureau of Accounting and Statistics, 1950.

Several factors account for the rapid expansion of trade between Taiwan and Japan: (a) additional basic foods had to be imported to Japan due to her rapid industrialization; (b) Taiwan could fulfill Japan's potential demand for agricultural products; (c) relaxed Taiwanese customs duties for imports from other areas led to a favorable climate for imports from Japan; (d) exports of basic foods to Japan was closely related to the development of plantation agriculture as well as that of the Taiwanese peasant agriculture; (e) the modernization of Taiwan's peasant agriculture, which would result from the influence of Japanese industrialization, would benefit from imports of capital goods and modernized production inputs. The last two items also constituted the motivating force behind autonomous development of agriculture and industries in Taiwan. This resulted in a more rapid growth of agriculture in Taiwan than in other South Asian colonial countries, which usually exported only one or two specific agricultural products. As a result of rapid expansion of trade between Taiwan and Japan, the total production of Taiwan relied increasingly on exports to Japan which increased from 11.5 percent in 1903 to 50.2 percent of total national production in 1934. The total consumption within Taiwan relied on imports from Japan. They increased from 13 percent in 1903 to 38 percent of total consumption in 1934. The dependence of the economy on exports to Japan was generally less than its dependence on imports before 1918. This situation altered significantly after 1918 as Taiwan changed from being a market for Japanese industrial goods to being a supplier of basic foods.[3] Rice, sugar, bananas, and pineapples were the most important agricultural products exported to Japan; sugar, bananas, and pineapples

[3] Takahashi, *op. cit.,* p. 313.

were specialized products, and rice was the mainstay of the agricultural production in both Taiwan and Japan. However, the production cost of rice in Taiwan was only about 57 percent of that in Japan.

Comparative advantage for rice production in Taiwan can be accounted for by low cost of wages and other expenses. Comparing the production cost or living expenditure of farm labor, per capita per year living expenditure was $Y = 135.68$ in Japan compared with $Y = 99.56$ in Taiwan in 1939. It is clear then that rapid expansion of agricultural exports to Japan in this period was attributed to the comparatively low wages and living expenditure in Taiwan.

International Trade in the Period 1950–1960

Since restoration from Japan in 1945 and separation from mainland China in 1950, Taiwan, economically independent, has faced several new problems in international competition. The favorable conditions which prevailed in the trade between Taiwan and Japan in the prewar period no longer existed (Table 28). Taiwan was not an exception to the rule of import surplus and dollar shortage which characterized most less-developed countries. Reconstruction of agriculture and industry from war damage and subsequent efforts for their further development required large imports of capital goods and raw materials. Quick recovery of agricultural production and expansion of agricultural exports had to be of primary concern in order to meet the foreign exchange requirements. However, the rapid expansion of domestic food consumption with a fast increase in population caused agricultural exports to decline. Exports and imports during 1950–1955, valued in 1935–1937 prices, were far below the level in 1911–1915 (Table 28). Value of exports during 1956–1960 was also below the 1916–1920 level. The gap in foreign exchange could only be met by United States economic aid. The important measures undertaken for foreign exchange adjustment were import restriction, employment of differential exchange rate, allocation of foreign exchange, and export promotion with trade agreements and state trading. Actually, these policy measures varied through the period according to changes in the balance of payment.

Table 28. International trade of Taiwan, 1911–1960
(in T$millions at 1935–1937 value)

Period	Value of import	Value of export	Trade balance
1911–1915	95	106	11
1916–1920	102	143	41
1921–1925	118	177	60
1926–1930	184	249	65
1931–1935	224	315	91
1936–1940*	288	377	90
1950–1955	76†	74	(−)2
1956–1960	130	128	(−)2

Source: Same as Table 27; also Economic Research Center, Council for United States Aid, *Taiwan Statistical Data Book* (Taipei, Taiwan, 1960), pp. 113–114.
 * For years 1941–1949 see asterisked note, Table 1.
 † Includes United States aid.

Roughly speaking, two periods can be distinguished by their different policy measures: (a) the period 1950–1957 in which the differential exchange rate and state trading were adopted with a view to restricting imports and allocating foreign exchange, and (b) the period since 1957 during which emphasis has been changed to encourage exports by means of area trade agreements and other diplomatic relationships. The real exports grew at 5.5 percent annually and imports at 5.8 percent from 1951 to 1961. These rates are much lower than the growth rate of GNP, which was 7.4 percent per year in the same period.

The most noticeable change in Taiwan's international trade in this period from that of the prewar period was the decrease in commodity and geographical concentration. For instance, agricultural products and processed products decreased from about 87 percent of total exports in 1939 to 68 percent in 1960.[4] More than 80 percent of trade dependency on Japan in the prewar period decreased to only 37 percent in total exports and 35 percent in total imports. The expansion of industrial production and diversification of agricultural production led to a certain degree of import substitution, and checked import demand to some extent. At the same time, the share of capital goods and raw materials in total imports increased from 65 percent in 1951 to 75 percent in 1960.

In view of the various efforts made for expansion of foreign trade, the change in its pattern and trend were quite encouraging. Nevertheless, the deficit in the balance of trade which was mainly covered by United States aid still lasted up to the recent period. More than one billion dollars of United States economic aid flowed to Taiwan between 1950–1960. It constituted 43 percent of the gross investment and accounted for nearly 90 percent of the flow of external capital and donation.

Agricultural Exports in Foreign Trade

Agricultural exports in this period can be separated into state trade and civilian exports. Exports of sugar and rice were managed under government control through collec-

[4] Economic Research Center, Council for United States Aid, "Taiwan Statistical Data Book" (Taipei, Taiwan, 1960), pp. 113–114, for statistical data on the percentage distribution of exports of Taiwan.

tion from farmers. The quantity of sugar exported was more or less fixed at 700,000 M/T annually under the quota from the International Sugar Agreement allocated to Taiwan. The quantity of rice exported was reduced to an average 100,000 M/T per year and fluctuated annually according to domestic production and the amount of government stockpiling. Exports of both products were generally made in accordance with some special trade agreement at a given price. For instance, a trade agreement with Japan was bilaterally set for limited exchange of rice and fertilizer at a given price. Export of sugar on the other hand was fixed in respect to quantity but was flexible in price. Civilian exports of agricultural products were for the most part carried on competitively in the international market. From the above observation, we might say that diversification of exports and decentralization of trading area gave the international trade of Taiwan a more competitive basis in this period. However, this indicates also that instability and price fluctuation of exports and imports can be reduced to some extent by increased trade diversification.

Price Fluctuations, Trade Stability, and Terms of Trade

Liang reported[5] that indices of trade instability and price fluctuation in Taiwan for the period 1951–1961 were rather moderate as compared with Coppock's findings.[6] The trade instability index was 18.95 for exports and 4.69 for imports, while the price fluctuation index was 7.66 for exports and 4.47 for imports. Coppock's estimate shows that the export

[5] Kuo-shu Liang, "Pattern of Trade and Economic Development in Taiwan, 1951–1961," *Industry of Free China*, Vol. 25, No. 4 (April 1966), pp. 41–42.

[6] J. D. Coppock, *International Economic Instability* (New York: McGraw Hill, 1962), pp. 49–50, 63–64.

instability index ranged from 73.8 to 6.2 for 83 countries during the period 1946–1958, and its median was 19.4. The import instability index for 83 countries ranged from 50.7 to 9.6, and its median was 20.5. Price fluctuation in Taiwan was relatively higher in case of exports than imports. The considerable amount of U.S. aid in the form of agricultural surplus might have contributed to the price stability of imports. Comparing Liang's estimate of price fluctuations in Taiwan with Michaely's findings about 36 countries in the period 1948–1958, the average of the latter amounted to 10.4, which was much higher than in Taiwan.[7]

With larger price fluctuations in exports than in imports, net terms of trade were kept almost constant first and then showed a declining trend (Table 29). Quantum index of

Table 29. Net terms of trade and export quantum index, 1952–1960
(1961 = 100)

Period	Unit value index		Net terms of trade	Export quantum index	Income terms of trade
	Imports*	Exports			
1952	114	130	114	59	68
1953	103	116	112	89	100
1954	111	121	108	62	67
1955	115	128	111	76	86
1956	109	121	111	74	82
1957	114	134	118	86	101
1958	109	115	105	105	111
1959	102	105	102	99	101
1960	103	98	95	97	93

Source: Department of Statistics, Ministry of Finance, Trade Statistics, Taipei, Taiwan, 1952–1960 editions.
* Includes United States aid.

[7] M. Michaely, Concentration in International Trade (Amsterdam: North Holland Publishing Company, 1962), pp. 70–72.

exports maintained an increasing trend except for 1959 and 1960. Income terms of trade or capacity to import has shown an increasing trend as a result of favorable or only slightly declining terms of trade and rapidly increasing exports.

Lyu and Liu have estimated the export function of Taiwan by using terms of trade and GNP during the period 1956–1960 as variables.[8] The estimated model is expressed by the formula:

$$Y = 121.63 + 0.9852X_1 + 0.0037X_2 \qquad R^2 = 0.98$$

where Y indicates the United States dollar value of exports, X_1 stands for terms of trade, and X_2 represents domestic GNP. The above export function indicates that 1 percent increase in the terms of trade is accompanied by 0.9852 million U.S. dollars of increase in exports, given constant GNP. When there is one million NT dollars of change in GNP, value of export will change by $3,700 (U.S.) assuming constant terms of trade. The export function tells us that expansion of exports heavily depends on improvement in the terms of trade and on increase in domestic production.

The expansion of agricultural exports in this period might be thought of as being due to agricultural diversification, improvement in terms of trade, and rise in agricultural productivity. In particular, development of new lines of foods with high income elasticity, such as oranges, mushrooms, onions, and pineapples, was important in boosting agricultural exports.

[8] Fu-chi Lyu and Tai-yien Liu, *T'aiwan mou-i chiao-i t'iao chien* (in Chinese) [The Terms of Trade in Taiwan] *Industry of Free China,* Vol. 20, No. 2, 1961, pp. 10–11.

Bibliography

Books and References

Bank of Taiwan. *T'aiwan ti shui-li* (in Chinese) [Irrigation Problems in Taiwan], *T'aiwan yen-chiu ts'ung kan* (in Chinese) [Special Series No. 4]. Taipei, Taiwan, 1950.

Barclay, George W. *Colonial Development and Population in Taiwan.* Princeton, New Jersey: Princeton University Press, 1954.

Chang, H. Y. "'T'aiwan nung-ming sheng chi yen-chiu" (in Chinese) [A Study on Farmer's Living Expenditure], *T'ai yin chi-k'an* (in Chinese) [Quarterly Journal of Bank of Taiwan], Vol. 8, No. 4, Taipei, Taiwan (December 1956).

Chang, Han-yi, and Ramon H. Myers. "Japanese Colonial Development Policy in Taiwan, 1895–1960: A Case of Bureaucratic Entrepreneurship," *Journal of Asian Studies,* XXII, No. 4 (August 1963).

Chen, Hong-yen. *Taiwan no keizai to nōgyō* (in Japanese) [Economy and Agriculture in Taiwan]. Taipei, Taiwan, Taiwan Shinpo Shia, 1944.

Chu, M. T. "Fei-liao huan-ku chih-tu ti chien-t'ao" (in Chinese) [An Assessment on Fertilizer Barter System] *Nung-you,* (in Chinese) [The Farmers], No. 3. Taipei, Taiwan, 1962.

Coppock, J. D. *International Economic Instability.* New York: McGraw-Hill Book Company, 1962.

David, P. A., and T. H. Vard de Klundert. "Biased Efficiency Growth and Capital-Labor Substitution in the United States, 1899–1960," *American Economic Review,* Vol. 55 (June 1965).

Erlich, Alexander. "Preobrazhenski and the Economics of Soviet

Industrialization," *The Quarterly Journal of Economics,* Vol. LXIV, No. 1 (1950).

Fei, John C. H., and Gustav Ranis. "Agrarianism, Dualism, and Economic Development," *The Theory and Design of Economic Development,* ed. Irma Adelman and Eric Thovbecke. Baltimore: Johns Hopkins Press, 1966.

———. *Development of the Labor Surplus Economy, Theory and Policy.* New Haven: Yale University, The Economic Growth Center, 1964.

Georgescu-Roegen, Nicholas. *Analytical Economics.* Cambridge: Harvard University Press, 1966.

Hsieh, S. C., and T. H. Lee. "Agricultural Development and Its Contributions to Economic Growth is Taiwan," *Economic Digest Series No. 17.* Taipei, Taiwan: Joint Commission on Rural Reconstruction, April 1966.

———. "An Analytical Review of Agricultural Development in Taiwan—An Input-Output and Productivity Approach," *Economic Digest Series No. 12.* Taipei, Taiwan: Joint Commission on Rural Reconstruction, July 1958.

Hsu, C. Y. "Rural Taxation in Taiwan." Taipei, Taiwan: Joint Commission on Rural Reconstruction, unpublished mimeograph, 1952.

Ishikawa, Shigeru. *Economic Development in Asian Perspective.* Tokyo: Kinokuniya, 1967.

———. "Kaihatsu katei ni okeru nōka rōdō jikyū" (in Japanese) [Farmers' Labor Supply in the Development Process], *Keizai Kenkyū,* Tokyo (January 1965).

Jensen, B. M. *Rice in the Economy of Taiwan.* Taipei, Taiwan: Report for FAO Mutual Security Mission to China, August 1953.

Johnston, Bruce F. "Agricultural Productivity and Economic Development in Japan," *Journal of Political Economy,* December 1951.

Joint Commission on Rural Reconstruction. "Food Administration in Taiwan," *Economic Digest Series No. 3.* Taipei, Taiwan, 1953.

Jorgenson, D. W. "The Development of Dual Economy," *Economic Journal,* June 1961.

Kawano, Shigeto. *Taiwan beikoku keizai don* (in Japanese) [Rice Economy of Taiwan]. Tokyo: Yuhikaku, 1941.

Kitayama, Tokujiro. "Utaka na Taiwan zaisei" (translated into Chinese [Wealthy Taiwan Finance] *T'aiwan ching-chi shi pah chi* (in Chinese) [Series of Taiwan Economic History No. 8], Taipei, Taiwan: Bank of Taiwan, 1957.

Kuznets, Simon. "Underdeveloped Countries and the Pre-Industrial Phase in the Advanced Countries," *The Economics of Underdevelopment,* ed. A. N. Agurwala *et al.* Oxford: Oxford University Press, 1958.

Lee, T. H. "Economic Analysis on Taiwan's Economy," unpublished lecture at National Taiwan University, Taipei, Taiwan, 1964.

———. "Intersectoral Capital Flows in the Economic Development of Taiwan, 1895–1960," Ph.D. thesis, Cornell University, Ithaca, New York, June 1968.

———. "Statistical Tables, Methodology, Data Sources, and Conclusions Regarding Intersectoral Capital Flows in the Economic Development of Taiwan, 1895–1960," Occasional Paper No. 11, Cornell University-USAID Prices Research Project. Ithaca, New York: Cornell University, Department of Agricultural Economics, 1968.

———. "A Study on Structural Change of Agricultural Production in Taiwan," *Agricultural Economic Seminar Proceedings.* Taipei, Taiwan: National Taiwan University, 1958.

———. "T'aiwan mao-chu chia-ke ti yen chiu" (in Chinese) [A Study on Hog Price in Taiwan] *T'ai Yin chi k'an* (in Chinese) [Quarterly Journal of Bank of Taiwan], Vol. 8, No. 3, Taipei, Taiwan (1956).

———. "T'aiwan ti nung-t'san chia-ke" (in Chinese) [Agricultural Prices in Taiwan] *T'ai Yin chi k'an* (in Chinese) [Quarterly Journal of Bank of Taiwan], Vol. 12, No. 2, Taipei, Taiwan (June 1961).

Lee, T. H., and H. T. Chen. "T'aiwan nung-yeh so teh fen-p'ei kou tsao" (in Chinese) [Distribution of Agricultural Income in Taiwan] *Ho-tsuo chieh* (in Chinese) [Cooperative No. 26]. Taipei, Taiwan: Cooperative Bank of Taiwan, 1958.

Lewis, A. B. "The Rice-Fertilizer Barter Price and the Production of Rice in Taiwan, Republic of China," *Journal of Agricultural Economics,* No. 5, Taichung, Taiwan (June 1967).

Lewis, W. A. *The Theory of Economic Growth.* London: George Allan and Unwin Ltd., 1955.

Liang, Kuo-shu. "Pattern of Trade and Economic Development in Taiwan, 1951–1961," *Industry of Free China,* Vol. 25, No. 4 (April 1966).

Lyu, Fu-chi, and Tai-yien Liu. "T'aiwan mou-i chiao-i t'iao chien" (in Chinese) [The Terms of Trade in Taiwan] *Industry of Free China,* Vol. 20, No. 2 (1961).

Mellor, John W. *The Economics of Agricultural Development.* Ithaca, New York: Cornell University Press, 1966.

——. "Toward a Theory of Agricultural Development," *Agricultural Development and Economic Growth,* ed. H. M. Southworth and Bruce F. Johnston. Ithaca, New York: Cornell University Press, 1967.

Michaely, M. *Concentration in International Trade.* Amsterdam: North Holland Publishing Company, 1962.

Minami, Ryoshin. "Classical Approach to Economic Growth," *Keizai Kenkyū,* Tokyo (July 1965).

Nurkse, Ragnar. *Problems of Capital Formation in Underdeveloped Countries.* Oxford: Basil Blackwell, 1955.

Ohkawa, Kazushi. *Nōgyō no keizai bunseki* (in Japanese) [Economic Analysis of Agriculture]. Tokyo: Taimeido, 1954.

Ohkawa, Kazushi, and Bruce F. Johnston. "The Transferability of Japanese Pattern of Modernizing Traditional Agriculture," a paper presented for Conference of the Role of Agriculture in Economic Development at Princeton University, National Bureau of Economic Research, December 1967.

Ohkawa, Kazushi, and Henry Rosovsky. "The Role of Agriculture in Modern Japanese Economic Development," *Economic Development and Cultural Change,* Vol. IX, No. 1, Part II (October 1960).

Okuda, Iku, *et al.* "Oranda jidai Taiwan nōgyō" (in Japanese) [Taiwan's Agriculture in the Dutch Period], *T'aiwan ching-chi shih tsu'chi* (in Chinese) [Series of Taiwan Economic History No. 1]. Taipei, Taiwan: Bank of Taiwan, 1954.

Parsons, H. L. *Impact of Fluctuation in National Income on Agricultural Wages and Employment.* Cambridge: Harvard University Press, 1952.

Rada, E. L., and T. H. Lee. "Irrigation Investment in Taiwan," *Economic Digest Series No. 14.* Taipei, Taiwan: Joint Commission on Rural Reconstruction, 1963.

Ranis, Gustav. "The Financing of Japanese Economic Development," *The Economic History Review,* Vol. XI, No. 3 (April 1959).

Rosovsky, Henry. *Capital Formation in Japan, 1868–1940.* New York: Free Press, 1960.

Ruttan, V. W. *Considerations in the Design of a Strategy for Increasing Rice Production in South East Asia,* a paper presented at Pacific Science Congress Session on Modernization of Rural Areas, Tokyo, August 27, 1966.

Sen, A. K. "Some Notes on the Choice of Capital-Intensity in Development Planning," *Quarterly Journal of Economics* (November 1957).

Shen, T. H. *Planning and Production.* Taipei, Taiwan: Joint Commission on Rural Reconstruction, 1958.

Shih, Chien-shen, *et al.* "T'aiwan fei-liao huan-ku ti yen-chiu" (in Chinese) [An Appraisal of the Fertilizer-Rice Barter System in Taiwan]. Taipei, Taiwan: National Taiwan University, College of Law, 1961.

Shihomi, Shungi. "Keisatsu to keizai" (translated into Chinese) [Police and Economy] *T'aiwan ching-chi-shih tsu-chi* (in Chinese) [Series of Taiwan Economic History No. 1]. Taipei, Taiwan: Bank of Taiwan, 1954.

Shinohara, Miyohei. "Capital Formation in Japan," *Keizai Kenkyū* (Tokyo), Vol. 4, No. 1 (January 1953).

——. "Kōgyō no seichō-litu" (in Japanese) [Growth Rate of Industry], *Nihon keizai no bunseki* (in Japanese) [The Analysis of Japanese Economy], ed. Tsurn and Ohkawa. Tokyo: Keiso, 1955, Vol. 1.

Takahashi, Kamekichi. *Taiwan keizai gendai don* (in Japanese) [Modern Taiwan Economy]. Tokyo: Ganshodo, 1937.

Tang, H. S., and S. C. Hsieh. "Land Reform and Agricultural Development in Taiwan," *The Malayan Economic Review*, Vol. VI, No. 1 (April 1961).

Umemura, Matazi. *Chingin, koyō, nōgyō* (in Japanese) [Wage, Employment, and Agriculture]. Tokyo: Taimeido, 1961.

United Nations, Economic Commission for Asia and Far East. "Intersectoral Capital Flows in the ECAFE Countries," unpublished report, 1963.

——. "Relationship between Agriculture and Industrial Development: A Case Study in Taiwan," *Economic Bulletin for Asia and Far East*, Vol. 14, No. 1 (June 1963).

Vanek, J. "Toward a More General Theory of Growth with Technological Change," *Economic Journal* (December 1965).

Woytinsky, W. S., *et al. Employment and Wages in the United States.* New York: Twentieth Century Fund, 1953.

Yien, C. Y. "Lin-yeh fa-chan ch'u-i" (in Chinese) [Development Measures for Forestry Industry], *Industry of Free China*, Vol. 14, No. 1 (1955).

Statistics

Cooperative Bank of Taiwan. *Ho-tso t'ung-chi nien-pao* (in Chinese) [Annual Statistics of Credit Cooperatives], annual issue, Taipei, Taiwan.

Department of Statistics, Ministry of Finance. *Trade Statistics,* Taipei, Taiwan, 1952–1960 editions.

Directorate-General of Budgets, Accounts and Statistics, Executive Yuan. *National Income of the Republic of China, 1962 issue,* Taipei, Taiwan, 1963.

Economic Research Center, Council for United States Aid. "Taiwan Statistical Data Book," Taipei, Taiwan, 1960.

Joint Commission on Rural Reconstruction. "An Estimate of Agricultural Capital Formation in Taiwan, 1955–1961," Taipei, Taiwan.

———. *Statistical Review of Agricultural Financing in Taiwan and JCRR Contributions,* unpublished report, Taipei, Taiwan, December 1961.

———. Rural Economics Division. "Food Balance Sheet of Taiwan," 1935–1960, annual issue.

———. "Total Agricultural Assets," unpublished data, Taipei, Taiwan.

———. "Utilization of Agricultural Products," unpublished report, Taipei, Taiwan.

Taiwan Agricultural Census Committee. *Report on the 1956 Sample Census of Agriculture,* Taipei, Taiwan, August 1959.

———. *Taiwan Agricultural Census Report for 1960,* Vol. 1, 1961.

Taiwan Governor General's Office. *Kōchi shoyu to keiei chōsa* (in Japanese) [Survey on Distribution of Landownership and Farm Management], Taipei, Taiwan, 1921.

———. *Nōgyō kinyū chōsa hōkoku* (in Japanese) [The Report on Agricultural Credit], Taipei, Taiwan, 1933.

———. *Taiwan beikoku seisan-hi chōsa* (in Japanese) [Survey Report on Rice Production Cost], Taipei, Taiwan, 1928.

———. *Taiwan jei-mu nen-pō* (in Japanese) [Annual Report of Taxing], Taipei, Taiwan, 1937.

———. *Taiwan jijō* (in Japanese) [Taiwan Situation], Taipei, Taiwan, 1927.

———. *Taiwan nōgyō nen-pō* (in Japanese) [Taiwan Agricultural Yearbook], 1901–1940 editions, Taipei, Taiwan.

———. *Taiwan nōka no seikei-hi chōsa* (in Japanese) [Food Consumption Survey on Taiwan Farm Families], Taipei, Taiwan, 1932.

———. *Taiwan nōka shu-shi keizai chōsa hōkoku* (in Japanese) [The Economic Survey on Farm Family Expenditure], Taipei, Taiwan, 1922.

——. *Taiwan sangyō kumiai yōran* (in Japanese) [Report on Industrial Cooperative], Taipei, Taiwan, 1918–1940 editions.

——. *Taiwan tō-kei sho* (in Japanese) [Taiwan Statistics], Taipei, Taiwan, 1896–1937 editions.

Taiwan Governor General's Office, Bureau of Finance. *Taiwan jei-mu hōkoku* (in Japanese) [Survey Report of Taxes], Taipei, Taiwan, 1933.

Taiwan Provincial Bureau of Accounts and Statistics. *Statistics of Taiwan's International Trade for 53 Years,* Taipei, Taiwan, 1950.

——. *T'aiwan nung-ming so-teh so-fu chia-keh chih shu* (in Chinese) [Indices of Prices Received and Paid by Farmers], Taipei, Taiwan, monthly issue, 1950–1960.

——. *T'aiwan t'ung-chi yao-lan* (in Chinese) [Taiwan Statistical Abstract], Taipei, Taiwan, 1950–1960 editions.

Taiwan Provincial Department of Agriculture and Forestry. *Nung-yeh shin yon t'iao cha* (in Chinese) [Report on Agricultural Credit], Taipei, Taiwan, 1950, 1951, 1960 issues.

——. *T'aiwan nung-fei nien-pao* (in Chinese) [Business Statistics Yearbook of Taiwan Farmers' Associations], Taipei, Taiwan, June 1964.

——. *T'aiwan nung-yeh nien-pao* (in Chinese) [Taiwan Agricultural Yearbook], 1945–1960 editions.

Taiwan Provincial Department of Civil Affairs. *T'aiwan jen-kou t'ung chi* (in Chinese) [Population Statistics of Taiwan], Taipei, Taiwan, 1945–1960.

Taiwan Provincial Department of Finance. *T'aiwan t'sai-cheng t'ung-chi nien-pao* (in Chinese) [Finance Statistics of Taiwan], Taipei, Taiwan, 1946–1960 annual issues.

Taiwan Provincial Food Bureau. *Monthly Rice Accounting,* Taipei, Taiwan, 1950–1960.

——. *The Survey Report on Sale of Agricultural Products,* Taipei, Taiwan.

——. *T'aiwan liang shih yao lan* (in Chinese) [Taiwan Food Statistics Book], Taipei, Taiwan, 1846–1960.

Taiwan Provincial Government. *T'aiwan wu-shih-i nien lai t'ung chi* (in Chinese) [The Fifty-one Years Statistics], Taipei, Taiwan, 1946.

United States Department of Agriculture. *Changes in Agriculture in 26 Developing Countries,* Foreign Agricultural Economic Report No. 27 (1963).

United States Department of State, Agency of International Development. Mission to China, "Economic and Social Trends," unpublished mimeograph, Taipei, Taiwan, 1963.

Index

*Intersectoral Capital Flows in the
Economic Development of Taiwan, 1895–1960*

Designed by R. E. Rosenbaum.
Composed by Kingsport Press, Inc.
in 11 point linotype Baskerville 3 points leaded,
with display lines in Helvetica.
Printed letterpress from type by Kingsport Press
on Warren's No. 66 text, 60 pound basis,
with the Cornell University Press watermark.
Bound by Kingsport Press in Columbia Bayside Linen
and stamped in All Purpose Foil.

DATE DUE